Imprints from an Odyssey

A Young Man's Journey

By Roger Neumaier

This book is dedicated to my Mother, my Father, Sally Luther and Erling Larsen.

Preface to *Imprints from an Odyssey*

Homer's *Odyssey* is the account of Odysseus' ten-year return to Ithaca from the Trojan War. During his voyage, Odysseus was subject to the whims of the Greek gods and continually encountered obstacles that delayed his homecoming. Those obstacles, in fact, were lessons. Each contributed in a unique manner to his journey's completion. Each turned Odysseus into a larger person.

Imprints from an Odyssey shares vignettes from my four-year journey which began in 1971. I was seeking a home—no doubt blown by much softer breezes than the hero Odysseus—but none the less driven by, and at the whim of, the metaphorical Greek gods. As I moved from job to job and city to city, I had no camera. Having no photographs from that period, I now must describe the people and places I experienced as they are imprinted into my mind's eye. This book presents a series of those imprints. Please treat my recollections of places and people as if they were snapshots in a photo album.

While I am the central character in *Imprints from an Odyssey*, the book is not about me. It is a sequential series of 1970s portraits of special people and wondrous places, each of which has made an imprint on me and has had a deep influence on my life.

I hope you enjoy *Imprints from an Odyssey*.

Roger Neumaier

1—Commencement

Graduation approached. It was spring of 1971. I was making important decisions about my future. Most of my college classmates were carefully considering which graduate school offered the best opportunity for future professional success. My sights, however, were set on escaping the collegiate environment. I wanted to go out into what many of us students referred to as *the real world*.

I announced to my friends that I did not want to become a white-collar worker. I needed to travel; to explore; to deepen my life experience. Once I had stepped out into and experienced the world, I hoped to figure out who I was and what I wanted to accomplish.

*****

The most meaningful advice I received while attending Carleton College had come from a close friend named Raka Anak Agung. Raka, who was from Indonesia, had experienced more of life than any student I knew. His father had been the last king of Bali. Raka's brother had led Indonesian students in 1965 when they overthrew their country's strong-arm leader, Nkrumah Sukarno. During that revolution, Raka fought alongside his brother—throughout the violence.

One day in my junior year, I was feeling confused about how to proceed in my life. I asked Raka for advice. He responded, "Roger, you are going to have to find it within yourself."

I asked, "How will I know when I have found it?"

He smiled softly and said, "You'll know."

*****

After receiving my diploma, I decided I would travel to a city where I knew no one. I would find a low-paying blue-collar job and build a life. I imagined all the wonderful things that would happen. I would meet interesting people and see fascinating things. I was without fear. I hadn't considered that I might not be able to find a job—or maybe I wouldn't earn enough to pay my way—or that I might succumb to sickness or violence. I was ready for adventure.

I had grown up in the insulation of the nineteen-fifties and the superficial affluence of the nineteen-sixties. Now, it was the nineteen-seventies. Like so many of my generation, I was questioning the values that had surrounded me throughout my life. I hadn't figured out how to replace them. But I would figure that out later. I just knew that now I was ready to cast my fate to the wind.

I remembered Raka's sage advice. I was beginning my search for *it*—whatever *it* was. My approach was inspired by stories of adventurous young American men who rode the rails during the 1930s, going from town to town, searching for work; by tales of young Japanese Buddhists, studying to become monks, who hiked from monastery to monastery in search of wisdom; and by literary models that included Tom Joad of *The Grapes of Wrath*, Don Quixote and, of course, by Odysseus.

*****

During that final term of my senior year, I spent much of my time preparing for my great adventure. I sold my books, my camera and most of my possessions paying down college loans and having five-hundred dollars in my pocket with which to begin my journey.

My last important decision was the selection of a city in which I would live. In order to be thorough, I went to Carleton's library to research possible destinations. After what seemed like a great deal of thought (probably almost a day), I settled on a city I had visited in the spring of 1971 when I had hitchhiked there with my college friend, Russ. Seattle was beautifully situated near mountains and the ocean and its weather was mild.

I decided to find a job in Seattle working in a warehouse. (Doing what specifically? I hadn't finalized that yet. I needed to be flexible).

When I told my Uncle Harold about my plan to go to Seattle, he pointed out that since The Boeing Company's airplane sales collapsed, a severe recession had gripped Seattle. Harold told me that might make finding a job difficult. I checked it out. Harold was right. The last thing I needed to do was move to a city where I couldn't find work. Seattle became a no-go.

Once Seattle was out of the running, I returned to the library. After another intense day, I narrowed my choices to Albuquerque, New Mexico and Portland, Maine. While I had never been to either city, both had rich cultural histories, were medium sized and surrounded by natural beauty. I figured I couldn't go wrong. But which city would it be?

I asked Russ, "What do you think? Portland, Maine or Albuquerque?"

Russ encouraged me to go to Albuquerque at about the same time I had begun to lean towards Portland. I can't remember my rationale—or his—just that we ardently disagreed.

When I finally told Russ I would go to Portland, he said, "Well damn it, then, I'm going to Albuquerque."

I wasn't sure where that had come from. Russ hadn't shared what his plans were after college. I thought he was going to become a doctor. But no. Russ stuck with Albuquerque. A couple days after I headed out to Portland Maine, Russ hopped onto his bicycle; put his possessions in saddlebags resting over his rear bicycle wheel; and pedaled over twelve hundred miles from Minneapolis, through Denver, to Albuquerque.

*****

My mother and brother flew to Minneapolis from Denver for my graduation. They rode to the Carleton campus with my aunt, uncle and grandparents to attend the commencement ceremony. They were all proud I had gotten a college degree from a prestigious college like Carleton.

After the ceremony, I spent a week in Minneapolis with my family. During that week, I attended the marriage ceremony of two close friends, Jim and Liz. Their wedding was more than just an opportunity for me to celebrate their wedding. It was a chance to say goodbye to many of my closest college friends—and, I guess, to the manner in which I had lived my life to that point.

A week later, my mom drove me onto Interstate 35 just north of Minneapolis where I stuck out my thumb. I was hitting the road with all of my possessions stuffed into a backpack, with five hundred dollars in my pocket and with a spirit of adventure.

*****

I hadn't told my mom where I was heading. No one in my family knew.

Years later, my mom told me how painful it was for her as she drove away; watching me in her rearview mirror as I disappeared into the horizon. That was her son—on the side of a highway—with his thumb out—going away—to God knows where.

At the time, I understood it was hard for her. But I also knew that that journey was something I needed to do.

2—On the Road

I was alone, waiting for my first ride of the first leg of a great adventure. I had said goodbye to my college, my friends, my family and the life I had known. My plan was to hitchhike north through Duluth, then continue along the coast of Lake Superior. After that, I would travel across Ontario, into Quebec and down to Boston. From Boston, I would head north to Portland Maine—to begin my new life. Attached to my backpack were a tent and sleeping bag. Along the way, I intended to camp out whenever and wherever I could.

Part of the reason I had not told my family where I was going was because I didn't want to lock myself into Portland Maine. I might find a place to stay before I got to Portland. Maybe Montreal? Who knew what other opportunities might come along?

However, a more honest explanation of why I hadn't told my family where I was going is that I wanted to distance myself from the turmoil of my parents' divorce. They had separated from one another at the beginning of 1965 and ever since, their conflicts had been a dominant factor in my life. In many regards, my journey was a move away from that pain.

*****

Hitchhiking was a common form of transportation for young people in the late 1960s and early 1970s. But many drivers were afraid to pick up hitchhikers. So, to improve my chances of getting picked up, I always tried to dress and look non-threatening. That meant I wore clean, neat clothes and pushed my long hair up into a stocking cap.

While I waited to catch the first ride of a hitchhiking trip, there was always a fair amount of tension. Would it take long to get a ride? Will whoever picked me up be nice? How far would they take me? Then, after that first car pulled over to the side of the road and I had grabbed my backpack and run up to the car, my tension disappeared. My adventure had begun.

My strategy for successful hitchhiking was to establish eye contact with drivers of passing cars. Once eye contact was made with a driver, I stood a good chance that the car would pull over to the side of the road. After it stopped and I had stowed my backpack in the back seat, I would climb into the front seat and thank the driver for the ride. Then, as the driver pulled into traffic, our conversation would begin.

Conversations were different on each ride. The driver would start by asking me questions about myself. "Where are you going? Are you a student?"

Then, he generally turned the focus of the conversation to himself. It was my responsibility, as the hitchhiker, to be a good listener. The driver would tell me about the wonderful or terrible things that were happening in his life. I refer to "he" and "his life" rather than "she" and "her life" because I was rarely picked up by a woman.

Each person who gave me a ride had a different set of interests and expectations. Some told me about the great disappointments in their life. Others shared how painful love had been—how their wives had left them or their girlfriends had been unfaithful. Some men told me how smart they were and how successful they had been in business. A few were just lonely and wanted to chat.

7

Hitchhiking required dutiful listening. By giving me a ride, the driver had earned my respect and attention. Sometimes after an initial conversation, a ride turned into a quiet and peaceful time during which the driver was lost in his thoughts and I was free to do the same. But that was generally not the case.

On longer hitchhiking trips, I tried to travel about five hundred miles in a day. Most rides lasted more than a hundred miles, but many were not that long. The time between rides was peaceful. However, calling that time *peaceful* assumes the weather wasn't too cold, too hot, too rainy or too windy.

When a person hitchhikes, they give up control of their schedule and of their ability to control their environment. At the end of each day of hitchhiking, I was exhausted.

*****

It was still early in the day. I had passed through Duluth, Minnesota and was heading north along Lake Superior. I had promised to visit a young classmate named Sandy who lived in Grand Marais, Minnesota, a small town on the shore of Lake Superior. Sandy had invited me to visit her on my way north. I was thrilled. Sandy was petite and cute; a kind and gentle person. She had a turned-up nose and long perfectly parted light brown hair. We had never dated but I couldn't help but have a crush on her.

Sandy's parents ran the general store in Grand Marais. After I arrived at her home (it wasn't far from the State highway), she and I went for a walk. Sandy brought her small dog along with us. She told me she trusted her dog's judgment in people. Her dog seemed to like me. That made me feel good.

After saying goodbye to Sandy, I stood on the side of the highway, listening to the waves of Lake Superior pounding on the rocky shoreline, once again with my thumb out. For the first time on the trip, I had the strong feeling that I didn't really know what the hell I was doing. I felt empty.

*****

I spent that night in a city park in Thunder Bay, Ontario. When I arrived there after midnight, it had been dark, foggy and beginning to rain. I found an isolated corner of the park, set up my tent, rolled out my sleeping bag and immediately fell asleep. When I awoke the following morning, it was a sunny. I quickly learned I was not located in an isolated spot. People were strolling through the park—right next to my tent. I quickly rolled up my sleeping bag, packed my tent and was on my way.

Mornings on the trip were great. I would fix coffee at my campsite or pack up my stuff and look for a little coffee shop. That morning, I enjoyed coffee and a doughnut at a small cafe. After finishing my second cup of coffee and every morsel of my doughnut, I threw my backpack onto my back and was off into the day.

*****

I walked to the outskirts of town. After a half an hour wait, an eighteen-wheeler picked me up. The trucker took me three hundred miles. Several hours later, moments after he left me off, I was feeling very satisfied with the day—until I realized I had left my light poplin jacket on the truck. I battled briefly with regret. Then I took a deep breath and decided I'd gotten a long ride in exchange for an old jacket—a fair trade.

Most rides were not that long. The following day I was hoping to get to Ottawa, a 500-mile distance from the youth hostel where I'd spent the night. It was ten o'clock, raining and I was at an unlit highway intersection still fifty miles away from Ottawa. I stood in the dark on the side of the road, pointing a flashlight at my hand—hoping any drivers that came along would see me—understand that I was hitch-hiking and be sympathetic enough to give me a ride. I began to consider setting up my tent in the nearby woods when a big black Lincoln Mercury pulled over. Its driver turned out to be a senior minister in the Canadian Government. He was headed into Ottawa.

In Ottawa, the driver went out of his way to take me to a youth hostel located in a student dormitory at Carleton University (no relation to the college I had just graduated from). There, I was given my own room with an adjoining bathroom. What a luxury! The next morning, after a long hot shower and a wonderful—and free—breakfast, I was on my way to Montreal.

*****

As I traveled across Canada, I spent three nights in youth hostels. The Canadian Government's sponsorship of hostels offered a safe place to stay, a warm meal and an opportunity to connect with other hitchhikers. Their support of youth contrasted with many jurisdictions in the United States that treated hitchhikers like criminals.

*****

It only took a couple of hours to get to Montreal from Ottawa. My ride left me off in the central business district of the city. It was noon. As I crossed a busy downtown intersection, a guy with long blonde hair and a headband turned to me and said, "Hey man, need a place to crash?"

He was about my age and wore bell-bottom blue-jeans, a white cotton Indian tunic and a string of beads. The invitation must have been prompted by my long hair, blue jeans and overstuffed backpack—signs that I was hip and might need a place to stay. I gratefully said *yes*.

He gave me directions to a house about a half mile away, adding, "Tell the guys at the house, Dave invited you."

*****

In the late sixties and early seventies, the term *hippy* was often used. But the word meant different things to different people. A *hippy* could be a person who lived off the land or it could be someone who had dropped out of the mainstream culture and economy. Some people were called *hippies* because they used a lot of drugs; others because they were into health foods and refused to use any drugs. College students from affluent families with long hair and torn blue jeans were called *hippies* even though they often were not very hip. For those young people, the outfit really was just a costume.

That definition having been established, I can tell you that all of Dave's housemates and friends were hippies—even though each was an unusual and unique person.

Mike was Dave's friend from high school; now a college student enjoying his summer break. He had a full dark beard and a great sense of humor. Another friend from high school, Bobby, was a dragged out, drugged out speed freak. Bobby had lost control of his life. His teeth were full of cavities—a condition I have since learned is caused by taking methamphetamines. Bobby's girlfriend also lived there. Her name was Jill. Jill, a tall, buxom, and attractive redhead, used to be a stripper.

Another housemate, Tim, was an American who had deserted the Army to avoid a second tour of duty in Vietnam. Tim looked like he was sixteen years old, but was probably in his early twenties. He lived off of panhandling on Montreal's Saint Laurent Boulevard. Tim looked so young and played the role of a homeless teenager so well that he earned a pretty fair income from asking for handouts.

All of Dave's housemates welcomed me warmly.

*****

A couple of hours after I arrived, Tim asked if I wanted to explore Mount Royal Park. The park is five hundred acres of forests and gardens that surround Mount Royal, the small mountain in the center of the city. The French speaking City of Montreal was named after that mountain.

I told Tim I was game to explore the park.

Before we left, Tim pulled out a small piece of wax paper with about a dozen small oddly shaped pink tablets stuck onto it. He told me the tabs were acid; then peeled one of them off of the wax paper and swallowed it. He offered me a tab. I had never taken a chemical hallucinogen though I had smoked marijuana and hashish. I took the tablet and swallowed it.

By the time we arrived at the park, I was quite high. We walked up a steep path to the top of Mont Royal. The view from the pathway was stunning—a panorama of majestic trees, colorful flowers and, after a brilliant sunset, sparkling lights from the city.

We returned to the house at about ten that evening. I had become distrustful of Tim and was uncomfortable staying in a house where I didn't know anyone.

A little while later, Tim left the house. The other housemates were sitting in the living room, listening to music and smoking grass. When Mike heard I was worried and had taken one of Tim's pills, he told me, "You're feeling anxious because you're high from that tab. Just try to relax. It will wear off soon."

That was good to hear. But I still felt uneasy.

*****

About a half an hour later, a guy I hadn't met joined us. When he entered the living room, he shined a flashlight onto my face and said, "You're under arrest."

I was stunned. Mike quickly explained to this guy that I was high. The guy said, "Sorry fellow. I was just kidding—I had no idea you were high. I'm Paul; another of Dave's high school buddies.

Paul's shoulder length hair was parted in the middle. He had a carefully groomed dark goatee with a twisted handlebar mustache and, in his dark raincoat and black wire rim glasses, looked a little like a nineteenth century psychiatrist.

It was a little after midnight. The group, including me, decided to go to a restaurant for a late dinner. Tim must have left his piece of wax paper with pink tablets on it at the house because Dave, Bobby, Mike and Paul each swallowed one of the tabs. As we left the house, Bobby told us he was going to use a tab of acid as his identification. As he said that, he put one of the pink tablets, still on a torn piece of wax paper, in his wallet in front of his driver's license.

Paul's father worked for the railroad. With the intent of getting Paul away from the Montreal drug culture for the summer, his father had given him a round trip train ticket to Vancouver, British Columbia. That evening, Paul needed to go to his parents' home to pick up the train tickets. After stopping at a small diner for spaghetti, we climbed back into Mike's car and drove to Paul's parents' condominium.

Their large condominium complex had a sizeable swimming pool in a fenced-in courtyard. While Paul went up to his parent's condominium to get his passport and railroad ticket, Mike climbed into the courtyard, stripped down to his underwear and dived into the pool. The others followed him. There we were, at three-thirty in the morning, a group of stoned long-haired young people, having a good old time in a suburban condominium's swimming pool. We must have woken up a lot of residents who probably did not feel warmly toward young people with long hair—especially if they were swimming in their pool in the middle of the night.

When Paul returned, he warned us about how loud we'd been. We piled back into the car and drove off, laughing while listening to rock and roll booming out of the car's radio. We waved at people in each car we passed. As we went over a bridge and were waving at the car behind us, its overhead lights started flashing. Then, we heard a siren. We quickly realized we had been waving at a police squad car with two uniformed officers.

The officers explained they were responding to a complaint from a condominium resident. They requested we get out of the car. One officer interrogated each of us, one at a time, while the other officer announced he was looking for drugs and proceeded to carefully search the car. While the officers were fully occupied, Dave and his housemates were throwing marijuana joints and pink tabs off the bridge into a river.

14

The officer began to interview Bobby and asked him for his identification. Mike quickly said, "Bobby—you left your wallet in the car."

A confused Bobby walked with Mike toward the car supposedly to get his wallet. But the wallet was in Bobby's pocket. Mike reminded Bobby that he had put a tab of acid in front of his driver's license. That pink tab quickly joined the other tabs in the river.

Paul explained to the officers that we had not trespassed—his parents lived in the condominium building. After not finding any drugs in the car and giving us a stern warning, the police officers released us. I was relieved. Back in 1971, getting caught with any illegal drug was a serious crime and I had had no idea how Canadian authorities would have dealt with a young U.S. citizen with long hair who had broken the law.

We arrived at Dave's house at seven in the morning. In spite of being tired, I decided I should move on. An hour later, I was on the road, thumb out, headed for Quebec City.

*****

I stayed at a youth hostel in a park in the center of Quebec City. The hostel was a stone building named *La Petite Bastille*. It had served as a prison for most of its three hundred years. Even though its interior was dark and damp, it proved to be a good safe place to sleep.

The lush park around *La Petite Bastille* was teeming with young people speaking French and English. That afternoon, I met two sisters from California who were on their own adventure. They were touring North America in a Volkswagen Beetle. They were planning to leave for Boston the following morning. I asked if I could ride with them to

Boston if I paid for half of their car's gas. After a moment's huddled discussion, they told me I was welcome.

The next day, the two California sisters and I drove south through rural Quebec; then across Vermont into New Hampshire. It was a scenic ride that took us through lovely villages, into lush forests and past old farms. As the day progressed, it became clear to me that the sisters were worried I might harm them. They knew nothing about me. In a society full of violence towards women, I understood why they were afraid. But there wasn't much I could do to allay their fears.

The drive was taking longer than they had anticipated. We didn't get into New Hampshire until late at night and realized we weren't going to get to Boston that evening. We'd have to camp along the road. I had a tent and sleeping bag. They had sleeping bags. I offered to share my tent. I could see their anxiety. They consulted with one another for a while; then accepted my offer.

Early the next morning, I made coffee and hot cereal for us on my portable stove and we got back on the road. I could see their relief when they said goodbye to me in downtown Boston. I appreciated the ride and was sorry it had turned out to be so uncomfortable for them.

*****

I was tired, but impatient to get to my new home. So, rather than hitchhiking, I bought a ticket on a Trailways bus from Boston to Portland. My journey from Minnesota to New England was about to end. My life after college was about to begin.

3—Portland

It seemed like only minutes after I boarded the Trailways bus in Boston that I was stepping off of it at Portland's downtown bus station. I walked away from the terminal looking all around, stunned with the city's New England charm and picturesque harbor. Portland had a feeling of history. Many of its central district buildings looked like they dated back to the late nineteenth century. I was impressed with my new hometown. But it appeared to be more of a large town than a major city.

The day was sunny—but not to warm. After I had walked around for a while and decided I liked the city, I began to look for young hip people to ask about low-cost apartments and workplaces that might be hiring. A young bearded man rode past me on a Peugeot bicycle. He wore a dark blue fisherman's cap, patched blue jeans and a tattered old gray sweater. Since he obviously knew where he was going and seemed to be fairly hip, I stopped him and asked for advice about housing and job prospects.

The guy didn't respond with information about jobs. I later learned that he was skilled at avoiding work and had no information to share on that front. But he did suggest an area to explore for an apartment. Then he got back on his stylish bike and rode off. It took me only ten minutes to walk to the neighborhood he'd recommended. The guy certainly had good taste. The area's apartment buildings were attractive and well-maintained 1920s vintage structures. I spotted a couple of for-rent signs and spoke with building residents. I learned that apartments in that hip and attractive area cost more than I could afford. I had hoped to spend between fifty and seventy-five dollars a month but the rent for a small apartment in that neighborhood was more than double that. The bearded bicycle guy certainly had an excellent eye for quality—and probably more money than me.

*****

I picked up a local newspaper and found an ad for a small apartment for fifty-five dollars a month. I called the building owner from a pay phone and met him at the apartment. The building was an unadorned, turn-of-the-century three story house that had been divided into six small apartments. It was located in a lower middle-class neighborhood, right next-door to a small pub.

The owner showed me the third-floor apartment. It shared a bathroom with another unit and was comprised of a small kitchen and a small bedroom. It had no separate living room. The kitchen was furnished with two old wooden chairs and a small well-worn wooden table. The bedroom had an old metal frame bed, a mattress and a dresser. The apartment was dingy and had a big hole punched into the kitchen wall. But each room had a window with a view of Portland Harbor. The natural beauty of the harbor was probably taken for granted by the locals. But for somebody like me who had grown up on the prairies of Minnesota, the view was breathtaking. I was thrilled! The apartment had everything I needed—and I could afford it!

I had been in town for about two hours and had an apartment. Now, I needed to find a job. Since I had experience working in restaurants, I walked back into the downtown area and applied for a job at the City's largest and most luxurious hotel. By the end of the day, I not only had secured a place to live, I had been hired as a waiter at the Sheraton Eastland.

I felt like a million dollars.

*****

Later that day, as I walked back from the Sheraton Eastland to my new apartment, I saw a hip young couple riding bicycles. Their bicycle saddlebags told me that they had just gotten into town—probably after a long journey. The guy hollered out, "Any idea where I can get a job?"

Based upon his long hair and their apparent recent arrival, I decided they were kindred spirits. His name was Dan. He and his girlfriend had ridden their bicycles from Chicago. Dan knew as much about Portland Maine as I had known several hours earlier—nothing. But now, I was the expert! I told Dan about the Sheraton Eastland. He thanked me and said he would check it out.

That evening, I celebrated the day's success by going out to dinner. I went to a working-class diner in downtown Portland where I ordered fried clam strips and french-fries. I had never had clam strips before. After a large green salad with a huge dollop of thousand island dressing, my waitress brought a plate overflowing with fried clam strips and french-fries. It was the best seafood meal I'd ever had. Including tip, the dinner cost about three and a half dollars. That was fairly expensive for me, but worth it. I felt quite successful.

*****

A couple of days later, I started at the Sheraton Eastland. I wore the required dark pants, white shirt and black bow tie. (I had purchased them the prior day at the W.T. Grant Department Store in downtown Portland.) The restaurant completed my outfit with a green waistcoat jacket.

My new job was fairly easy to learn given that I had worked in the food service industry in the past. But restaurant work is intense. Waiters and waitresses are expected to move quickly, be friendly and communicate well. Successful waiters are highly organized and are not supposed to make mistakes. They set up their assigned tables, take orders from guests, serve meals, then deliver the check—and that check had better be correct. Waiters must be ready to respond to questions about the menu—and local tourist attractions—and appreciate the knee-slapping humor of stupid jokes. Above all, they must be able to ignore aggressive comments while delivering customer service to multiple tables at the same time. The complete cycle of table set-up, order taking, food serving and billing for each table repeats itself again and again as guests come and go.

Some waiters and waitresses worked at the Sheraton Eastland each summer season. In the fall and winter, they worked at resorts in warmer climates like Florida.

Because of seasonal staff turnover, the employees at the Sheraton Eastland did not have a strong sense of being a team. This lack of cohesiveness led to constant competition between waiters who sought the guests who tipped most generously. The most aggressive waitstaff constantly outmaneuvered other waiters. But there were many ways in which staff undercut one another.

For example, during breakfast rush, waiters were responsible not only for putting in orders for breakfast entrees and for serving coffee, tea and juice to their guests, they also toasted and buttered bread or heated muffins for each order. Oftentimes an aggressive waiter would grab toast for his table's guests—toast that had been put into the toaster by another waiter for their guests. When that second waiter's eggs, hashbrowns and bacon were ready to serve, they would find no toast in the toaster. That second waiter had to choose—either serve cold eggs, hash browns and bacon or bring the guests their toast or muffins several minutes after everything else had been served.

In either case, guests believed that that waiter whose toast had been taken was incompetent. Guests never had an idea about the politics occurring in the kitchen. I became familiar with sarcastic comments from customers after the toast I had started was served to a more aggressive waiter's table.

One time, after another waiter took my toasted English muffins, I took the English muffins put into the toaster by a third waiter. As I was buttering the muffins, he came up to me and humbled me for taking his muffins. As he took them from me, he said, "You should be ashamed of yourself—stealing from another waiter!" Of course, I felt awful.

The battle between staff was actually more complicated than the job responsibilities. I not only had to focus on doing my job, I had to keep an eye out for other waiters to make sure that they didn't undercut my efforts. When a customer wasn't happy, the restaurant's manager didn't care why. He just chastised the waiter whose guests complained.

*****

I wasn't the restaurant's only new employee. Two days after I started, Dan (who I had met as he biked into town from Chicago) began work at the Sheraton. He had listened to my suggestion of where to look for work.

*****

Each day, I was tired when I returned home after work. But I was proud to have my own place. Other than college residence halls, that apartment was my first home away from my parents. I made improvements to my place. I purchased a dark flowery piece of 1940's carpet at the Salvation Army store and used it to cover most of the bedroom floor. I placed the old metal bed frame in the building's basement and also put the mattress on the floor.

I purchased a complete set of *depression ware* dishes from the Salvation Army. These light blue pressed glass plates and cups had a detailed flower pattern impressed into them. With that purchase, I felt I had really scored. The complete set cost me less than ten dollars.

I finished outfitting my kitchen with a couple of old cast iron pans and an old-fashioned toaster. The toaster had probably been manufactured in the 1920s. Each of its sides was a stainless-steel door that folded out. I could place a piece of bread on one or on both of those side-doors. Then, after I pressed a black button on the toaster, the doors closed and the toaster heated one side of each slice of bread. After a couple of minutes, the toaster doors slowly opened and it flipped the pieces of bread over! I was amazed by how that little contraption created two almost perfectly toasted pieces of bread.

I purchased one item at the Salvation Army Store that was totally impractical—an old Bible that had deeply embossed designs on a thick leather cover. The bible's pages were decorated with ornate script and colored illustrations. On the front page were the handwritten names of the bible's original owner's family members. Each name had a birth and death date. The dates ranged between 1850 and 1890. While I was not religious and certainly not Christian, this beautiful book with such a meaningful history was an irresistible acquisition for only five dollars.

*****

Living on my own meant learning to do new things. I had never patched drywall. After I fixed the hole in the kitchen wall, I was so proud of my less than mediocre repair job. I'd never before picked a room color, let alone painted a room. I painted that kitchen a pastel peach color. Here again, after finishing the job, I was glowing more than the paint.

Cooking for myself was a new experience. During the first couple of weeks, my favorite homecooked meal was a fried half can of corned beef hash topped off with a fried egg. The meal was satisfying. I felt like a master chef!

But that was just a start for my gourmet exploration. Having read most of *Diet for a Small Planet,* a book about dining on non-meat proteins, I figured I should try it out. So, with only a modest understanding of the concepts in the book and without the benefit of any recipes, I went to town— so to speak.

I began by mixing grains and dairy—two food groups that were full of protein. For the dairy product, I bought a quart of soft ice milk from a nearby Dairy Queen. I put the soft ice cream on top of a wheat product, in this case a frozen Sarah Lee pastry from the local grocery store. Preparation was simple. I just heated the pastry in my oven; then put the ice milk on top of it. It tasted so good—and I was eating healthfully while preserving the planet!

For a week, most of my dinners were that ice milk/pastry combination. For a change of pace, I fixed a couple of meals with whole wheat toast, butter (thus combining whole grains and dairy per *Diet for a Small*

Planet) and honey (my grandmother had always told me that honey had special nutrients).

I felt I had found the perfect vegetarian cooking regime. But I started getting dizzy and running out of energy at work. I countered that a little by eating lunches of the Sheraton Eastland's clam chowder. After a while, I became suspicious that my dinners of Dairy Queen ice milk, Sara Lee pastries, whole wheat toast, butter and honey might be the problem. I returned to hash and eggs.

*****

My time away from work was spent in silence. I didn't have a radio, stereo or television and attended no movies while living in Portland. My days were spent walking around the city. People in Maine were more reserved than any group I had encountered. It was difficult to meet them and even more difficult to get to know them. Bottom line, I wasn't making any friends in Portland.

In college, I had short relationships with women. But I held back from making any long-term commitments. In retrospect, my fear was likely driven by having watched the pain of my parents' marriage—pain they generously shared with my brother, sister and me.

However, fear of a relationship never stopped anyone from wanting one. At the Sheraton, I worked with two young women, Kate and Julia. They were hired as waitresses about the same time I was. Julia was exuberant and talkative. Kate was subdued, smart and cute. I had a crush on Kate. But I was pleased to be making friends with both of them. I invited them to have tea at my apartment. They liked my place. Julia told me if I ever gave it up, I should let her know. She wanted to move out of her mother's home and liked my apartment (and its low rent).

Kate invited me to a picnic at her family's cabin on Lake Sebago—about 30 miles from Portland. It was a wonderful Saturday. The sun was shining, the lake was big and deep, and I felt totally included by her family.

But those couple of visits were exceptions. I spent almost all of my time by myself.

*****

Portland is a beautiful little city. When I wasn't at work, I often walked through its neighborhoods of old clapboard houses and charming parks. That is what I was doing on the Fourth of July. It was sunny and I had decided to celebrate by going for a walk.

A woman wearing a dark drab cotton house-dress walked up to me. Her thin face was marked with the deep wrinkled lines of a hard life. She cried out, "Help me. My daughter won't let me to enjoy the holiday."

Based on how the woman staggered and slurred her speech, I realized she was drunk. Following her, and obviously embarrassed and overwhelmed by the situation, was her daughter who was probably less than twenty years old. The daughter, dressed in blue jeans and a plaid shirt, also asked for my help. "This is not the first time mom has drunk too much and won't come home. Can you help me, please?"

My heart went out to her.

We flagged down a Yellow Cab. I tried to talk the mother into getting into it. She insisted she would not get in the cab unless I accompanied them. So, the three of us rode to their home, the first-floor flat of a dingy white clapboard house. I helped the daughter get her mother into a simply furnished living room. While the daughter put her mother to bed, I waited with her seven-year-old brother.

At about 5 o'clock, the daughter returned to the living room. Her mom had finally fallen into a deep sleep. She told me she was going to take her brother to a nearby park to watch Fourth of July fireworks over Portland Harbor. "Would you come along with us—I mean, share our picnic supper—and watch the fireworks?"

I had never liked fireworks. But having been so insulated from human contact, I was thrilled to spend the evening with someone. We got to the park that overlooked the harbor's wharf well before sunset. The young woman rolled out a blanket and the three of us sat down and enjoyed cold fried chicken, potato salad and root beer. Afterwards, I was surprised how much I enjoyed the fireworks. It had turned into a wonderful evening. I walked them back to their home, then said goodbye.

I never saw them again.

*****

During winter term of my senior year at Carleton, I had taken a course in *Zazen* or sitting meditation. It was taught by Nishan-San, a Buddhist monk who was a one-term guest of the college from Japan. Classes for the three-month, five day a week course began each morning at six in a small gymnasium. For the first twenty minutes of each day's session, students would meditate—sitting in a cross-legged yoga pose. Then for twenty minutes, Nishan-San would speak to us, telling us stories about Buddhism and life. For the final twenty minutes of each morning's class, we again meditated.

I remember Nishan-San saying, "In twenty or thirty years, each of your lives will have become complicated. There will be times when you feel overwhelmed. When that happens, you will remember what Nishan San said. You will meditate."

Nishan San was right—but it didn't take twenty or thirty years. During that summer, I meditated often. Meditation has been a personal tool for finding peace—in Portland—and in each place I have lived since. It's helped me deal with life's challenges.

*****

I visited the small corner pub next-door to my apartment building at least once a week. It was a long narrow room with windows along one side and a long wooden bar with a dozen barstools on the other. When I visited, there were usually five or six men sitting at the bar—never anyone less than fifty years old. Even though I never really got to know anyone at the pub, the bartender and his regulars treated me kindly. I would enter, sit down on a barstool and instantly be a part of whatever conversation was taking place—all for the twenty-five-cent price of a schooner of beer.

One afternoon, a woman in her sixties joined us at the bar. The moment she sat down; the regulars started teasing her. She took it all in good humor. When she left, I asked the others: "Who was that lady?" They all laughed at me for having asked that question.

Then the bartender explained their laughter. "That's no lady." And then, as a group, they again roared with laughter.

I understood that to them, the word *lady* must have meant someone of a higher class. But the woman was their friend. She liked them. And in spite of all their teasing, I could see they liked her as well. She was one of them—a part of their economic and social class. I think their discomfort in calling her a *lady* wasn't a comment on her as much as it was a statement about their images of themselves.

*****

Speaking of economic and social classes, I felt like I had officially joined the working-class—and I was proud of it. It felt good to be self-sufficient and earning an honest living. And I must have come off as a working-class person to the college students on summer break and young professionals who I ran into around town. They treated me as if I was from a lower class. I accepted that, making a personal judgement that they were arrogant and superficial.

In retrospect, I know I was *not* working-class. I had just completed a wonderful education at a prestigious college. My parents had instilled in me the confidence to explore the world as an adventurer rather than a need to immediately secure a career to survive. I had a freedom that was not available to most. For example, the young woman I met on the Fourth of July who was taking care of her drunken mother—she didn't have the freedom I enjoyed.

*****

In mid-July, I scheduled five consecutive days-off from work to visit my friends in Montreal. After hitchhiking there and spending a couple of satisfying days with Dave and his housemates, I headed back to Portland. On the return trip, I passed through the City of Sherbrooke, Quebec and visited Mary, a friend from college. Mary had gotten married in 1970, shortly after graduating. When I wrote to her earlier in the summer, she invited me to spend a night in their home.

Mary and her husband treated me royally. However, it saddened me to see the extent to which Mary's macho husband treated her like a child. He condescended to her throughout the meal. I remembered her as such a bright and articulate woman—always positive, independent and kind. Because I was a man, her husband treated me with respect in a stark and almost embarrassing contrast to how he treated his wife.

The next morning—since I am such a diplomatic person—I told Mary what I thought of her husband's behavior. She was hurt and offended. In spite of a letter of apology sent to her later in the summer, I have not heard from her since.

*****

After bidding adieu to Sherbrooke, I hitchhiked through the agricultural back country of French Quebec. At one point, unable to catch a ride, I spent an hour on a gravel road in the middle of nowhere. A tractor finally came by pulling a farm wagon loaded with hay. The farmer invited me to hop onto his hay wagon which I did. Then, for about two miles, I had my own little hayride.

The farmer left me off at a rural intersection two miles south of the middle of nowhere near a small coffee shop. I decided I could use a break. The coffee shop was right out of the early nineteen-fifties. It had three small chrome and red Formica covered tables, each with matching chrome and vinyl chairs. Its white Formica counter had four or five chrome and red vinyl stools.

I sat down at a stool and asked for a cup of coffee from the woman behind the counter. There was a strawberry pie sitting in a glass case behind her which looked inviting. I asked, "Is that pie good?"

She responded in English with a strong French-Canadian accent, "I picked the strawberries this morning."

I asked for a piece of the pie. It turned out to be the most wonderful pie experience of my life. After finishing that incredible slice of fresh strawberry pie, I spotted some chocolate chip cookies.

I asked her, "Are those cookies good?"

She responded, "I made them."

I have always felt that that short episode in an out-of-the-way café should be the gold standard by which all small coffee shops are measured.

*****

I got back onto the road, but did not catch a ride. So, I walked, passing a farm with several horses grazing in a pasture. I was intrigued. Would the person who owns those horses let me let me ride one for a few dollars? I walked up a long driveway to an old farmhouse. A farmer was working on a tractor in the barnyard. Since this was French Quebec, I knew that if I wanted to speak with him, I should do so in the French language.

Good news and bad news often accompany one another. Speaking French was the right decision. Turns out the farmer did not speak any English. The bad news was that I did not speak French very well. When I asked if I could rent a horse for a ride, I used the word *cheveux* (meaning hair) instead *chevaux* (meaning horses). A literal translation of what I said is, "Would you be willing to allow me to ride one of your hairs if I paid you?"

Fortunately, the farmer was not offended. I think he understood that I just couldn't speak the French language very well. But he probably felt—and arguably he was correct—that I was an idiot. I left that farmyard with no response—just a look—from the farmer.

I returned to the gravel road to continue my journey. The rest of the trip back to Portland was pleasant and without event.

*****

In late July, I wrote a letter to my sister Diane who lived in Chapel Hill, North Carolina. It was my first communication with a member of my family since leaving Minneapolis six weeks before. I told Diane where I was living and what I was doing. She wrote back telling me that both my father and mother were worried about me. Diane's letter said I needed to let them know I was doing fine. I recognized she was right and promptly sent a letter to each of them.

In my letter to my mother, I explained why I had not been in touch with her. I told her I needed to focus on discovering who I was outside of the context of my family. I don't think my mom grasped that. The pain caused by her divorce from my father was just too great to allow her to see another person's perspective.

In my letter to my father, I talked about needing time by myself. My dad was an interesting and talented man; a holocaust survivor; an outstanding intellectual; and a very hard worker. At the time, he was President of the State University in New Paltz, New York. The only downside of all of his special qualities and responsibilities was that he hadn't had a lot of time for me, my sister or my brother. In my letter to him, I told him that since he was not available, I needed to stop trying to build the relationship. It was time for me to focus on myself.

In some regards, my letters amounted to late adolescent whining. But the letters were more honest than I'd ever been with my parents. I felt it was important for me to communicate clearly to them—even if the message I was delivering was not one they wanted to hear.

*****

Each of my parents wrote back quickly—pleased that I was in touch with them and offering no recriminations for my seclusion or my justification for it as expressed in my letter. I was particularly surprised by my father's letter. He offered to visit me almost immediately; adding that if he had not been available for me, he regretted it. He wanted to communicate with me now. My father asked me to call him and set up a time for him to come to Portland to visit me.

His response seemed extraordinary. I phoned to let him know I would welcome such a conversation. He told me that he and my stepmother Sally would leave for Portland the following morning, a Saturday.

*****

My dad and Sally checked into a hotel late Saturday afternoon. Sally stayed at the hotel while my dad visited me at my apartment. In addition to restating much of what he said in his letter, he asked me to be honest with him and he would work to be responsive; to build our relationship. We spoke through most of the night. The conversation was an extraordinary event. My dad had often been too busy. Now, I was being offered as much time as I wanted. I told him I didn't need his time as much as I desired to know that he cared; that he was available.

That evening and the following day were two of the most important days of the summer. I was enriched by learning that my father loved me. Not only did I rebuild my relationship with him, but I learned something about life from his example of humility—his willingness to admit he wasn't perfect—and commitment to work to be responsive to me.

*****

I didn't read much during the first half of that summer. Tons of collegiate required reading had drained my enthusiasm for literature. However, as the summer progressed and with so much time available, I missed reading a good book. I was ripe to start reading again and the Portland Library offered an inviting location. Its ornate brick facade opened into a comforting interior of well-worn, almost century-old wooden floors, oak tables and matching chairs. The library emanated history.

I began to explore the library's collections and was rewarded with the discovery of a large group of books about Native Americans. I read a bunch of them. One book, *The Soul of an Indian,* was written by a Harvard educated Native American at the beginning of the twentieth century. Its author, Dr. Charles Alexander Eastman, born in 1858, was a member of the Santee Sioux Tribe. Eastman's book recounted memories from his childhood including stories told to him by his grandmother. The book emphasized the difference between the things Eastman had learned at Harvard and the spiritual guidance his grandmother had relayed to him—the wisdom that comes from being in touch with nature.

*****

I occasionally saw the bearded guy with the worn dark blue fisherman's cap who had spoken with me on my first day in Portland. While he had seemed to have more money than me, it is of note to mention the last time I saw him. He was panhandling in Portland's downtown area. I have never been judgmental of panhandlers—of war

33

veterans. But this guy seemed pretty affluent and he was definitely no veteran.

When I saw him panhandling, I told him he should be ashamed of himself. I think his response to my comment was that I just wasn't cool.

*****

The Portland wharf was a scenic composite of fishing boats; beautiful ancient warehouses and docks; and the harbor itself. One day in midsummer, I was walking along the wharf when I was approached by a short, stout, older man with thinning gray hair, mustache and goatee. Out of the blue, he asked if I needed a job. Being a waiter at the Sheraton Eastland was not exciting, but it had provided me with a stable income. However, I have always been a little curious regarding how green the grass might be on the other side of a hill.

The man introduced himself as Max. He told me his company provided crates to lobster boathouses on the wharf. Lobsters were shipped in those crates all over the world. Max's truck drivers drove to local supermarkets and collected the stores' discarded wooden slatted lettuce and vegetables crates. The grocery stores actually paid Max to haul the crates away. Max's employees brought the crates to an old warehouse on Portland's wharf. There they lined the inside of the crates with newspaper, then delivered them to small boathouses on the wharf where fishermen brought their freshly trapped lobsters. Lobsters were shipped all over the country in those crates.

Max needed a truck driver. I would drive a two-ton truck to the various grocery stores, pack and tie the crates onto the truck's bed and transport them back to the wharf. The job paid $1.75 an hour. Max explained that I would work

34

with one other employee. The job was available because the person who had been in the job for years, had taken up drinking and disappeared.

While I hadn't been looking for a job, how could I pass this up? The next day, I gave notice at the Sheraton Eastland. I had found the ideal job in the perfect city. I felt so successful!

*****

I started working for Max a few days later. For the first couple of days, Max or his son rode with me on my route, introducing me to grocers, informing me of what I needed to do and warning me about what I should avoid doing.

As he trained me, Max, in a Jewish New York accent, would explain his philosophy of commerce. "If you look around, you can always start a successful company—just by finding junk—stuff one person will pay you to haul away and another person will purchase from you. Recycling is an underappreciated business."

Max's son looked and sounded like a younger version of his father. However, his perspectives on commerce were different. He made it clear to me that he was never going to take over his father's business. Max's son was in law school. The sooner he stopped working for his dad, the better. It wasn't a matter of disrespect, he explained. He respected his father a lot. But Max's son wanted the white-collar life that I was trying so hard to avoid.

I learned the job. I drove up to a grocery loading dock; loaded, stacked and tied boxes onto the truck; then I headed for the next grocery store. I followed that routine until I couldn't fit another box on the truck. Then I brought the boxes into Max's warehouse on the wharf.

It turned out that driving the truck, picking up and delivering boxes was only a third of my new job. The rest of my time was spent working in the warehouse, lining wooden crates with newspapers. I worked with Max's other employee, Bob. Bob had worked for Max for decades. He was about sixty; a quiet guy who was constant in his effort. Bob never shared much about himself. He did tell me that the man I'd replaced had worked for Max off and on for a decade. Every year or two, this guy would take to drink and disappear for a month or two, only to return after he was out of funds.

Bob showed me how to line the lettuce crates with newspaper. I'd take a crate from the stack of unlined crates; set it down in front of me on a table; open it by swinging its top back; line the crate with two newspaper pages; line the top with another page; close the crate; and put it on the stack of lined crates. I repeated those steps for each crate; lining one crate after another; using the same steps at the same pace. The work had a rhythm and while we worked, we listened to a local rock and roll radio station. After hours spent lining crates while listening to the radio, several popular songs from the summer of '71 are deeply ingrained in my psyche. More than forty years later, when I hear Joan Baez singing *The Night They Drove Old Dixie Down* or Rod Stewart's rendition of *Maggie May*, I want to grab a crate and line it with newspaper.

*****

By the middle of August, I began to feel confident about my future in Portland. My only problem was that I didn't have any friends. I would be spending a lot of time by myself in the coming winter. Days would be shorter, it would be cold and when I wasn't working, I would be by myself. I needed a plan to deal with that.

I decided to get a pet.

I was not experienced in that area. My family had had only one pet, a pudgy cocker spaniel named Footsie. Footsie was sweet—to some of us. But she had the nasty habit of drawing blood from people she didn't know, particularly relishing small children's hands.

But I was resolved to forget about Footsie's bite and get a pet. I had always liked dogs more than cats. But a dog required a yard or regular walks. Cats, on the other hand—cats go to the bathroom inside your home—in a box. My problem was I really didn't trust cats. I had once been told by a girlfriend that I was shortsighted for not trusting cats (one of quite a few weaknesses she had been kind enough to point out).

Anyway, after about five minutes of thorough analysis, I decided to address that weakness and get a pet at the same time. I walked to a downtown Portland pet store to check out my options for feline friendship. About a half an hour later, I triumphantly marched out of the store with a young gray Siamese kitten that had one green eye and one blue eye. In addition to the kitten, I purchased a bunch of cat stuff including food, litter, a litter box and a collar.

I christened my new kitten *Tiger*. Tiger was the largest personal commitment I had made since graduating from college. After arriving at home, I created a bed for Tiger. He showed his enthusiasm by scratching my arm.

About an hour later, Tiger disappeared. I panicked, trying to remember if I had left either the door or a window open. After about ten minutes of intense searching, I found Tiger asleep on top of a sweater in the bottom drawer of my bureau. He had climbed into the back of the drawer from underneath the bureau.

I was relieved—for a while.

Within a couple of hours, my arm began to develop welts. I became congested. I learned that in addition to not trusting cats, I happened to be allergic to them.

*****

One day, after about a month working for Max, he asked me to come into his small office in the back of the warehouse. There Max explained to me that the man I had replaced had sobered up. He had asked for his job back.

Max explained, "Let's be honest, Roger. You have a college education. You're just not going to stay here for the long haul. I need somebody who will. Sure, this guy gets drunk and disappears for a month or so every couple of years. But he is happy with the work; satisfied with the wages. He always returns. So, I don't need you anymore, Roger. I'll write you a check for the hours you worked this week and you can be on your way."

I told him he couldn't do that. I said federal law required him to give me two weeks' notice. I wasn't sure if that was the case or not, but Max didn't challenge my analysis of the law. He just said, "Okay. Fine. I'll find work for you to do."

He led me out of his office, up a set of wooden and dusty steps to the second floor of the warehouse. It looked like no one had been there in decades. There was about an inch or two of dust over everything.

Max said "You want two weeks work. Here. Clean up this second floor," and he gave me a garbage can, a broom, a dustpan and a shovel.

I spent about a half of an hour trying to attack the dust before deciding this was not turning into a winning proposition. If I was going to make Max employ me for another two weeks, he would make me miserable for all of that time.

I walked downstairs, found Max and said, "OK. Write me the check."

*****

It was almost the beginning of September. I didn't have a job. I had no friends and was facing a long cold winter. Julia had told me that if I ever left my apartment, she was interested in taking it. I stopped by the Sheraton Eastland and asked her if she still wanted it. She did.

A couple of hours later, after speaking with my landlord and getting my apartment deposit back, I started to put together a plan for life after Portland. But I had one more issue to resolve.

*****

Over my two weeks with Tiger, it had become abundantly clear that he was a sweet kitten. But it was just as clear that my allergy to cats was real. Even if I had stayed in Portland, I couldn't have kept him. Now that I was leaving town, I needed to quickly find a home for Tiger. I picked up the kitten, his bed, and all of his food and supplies and carried them downtown. It was five o'clock in the evening. Office workers' workdays were ending. Employees were leaving their workplaces and returning to their homes. I needed to find somebody who might like to have a very sweet little kitten.

I stood in front of an office building in downtown Portland holding Tiger in my arms, his cat paraphernalia in a bag at my feet. I watched people pass.

After about 20 minutes, I spotted a young woman who seemed to be kind. She was a candidate for Tiger's love. I walked up to her and told her that I wanted to give her my kitten. She was a little taken aback. But after I explained my circumstances, she became more comfortable that there wasn't a catch. She picked up Tiger, cuddled him a couple of times and said, "Yes".

Then she went away from me, holding the cat supplies in one arm and Tiger in the other. While she walked, she was talking to Tiger.

And Tiger seemed pleased.

4—The Appalachian Trail

It was early September of 1971. I had been fired, ended my apartment lease and trimmed my belongings down to what would fit in my backpack. My finances were in order and once again, I had more than five hundred dollars with which to begin a new life in some unknown city.

During my mid-summer trip to Montreal, I passed a point a couple of hours west of Portland where the Appalachian Trail intersects the state highway. At the time, I made a mental note that the Trail might be a fun hike for the future. Now, that future had arrived.

At a downtown Portland bookstore, I bought a book about the Appalachian Trail. From it, I learned that the Trail begins in northern Maine and goes all the way down to Georgia, passing through mountains and forests the entire way. I decided I would try to hike most of the trail, beginning where the state highway intersected with it. After the hike, I decided I would go to live somewhere near my sister Diane in North Carolina.

I had never gone on a long hike. But I have never let ignorance stand in the way of a challenge. The hike would be an amazing adventure! If I began it immediately and made good time, I could complete it before the trail was covered with deep snow.

I owned basic camping equipment. So, all I needed to purchase was food for my meals along the trail. During the summer, I had learned a lot about healthy foods and had a better idea of which foods provide the best nourishment. However, I still had not discovered that when one takes a long hiking trip, one should buy foods that can be cooked quickly and easily.

I went to the Portland food co-op and bought brown rice, whole wheat flour, and a variety of other healthy foods. I supplemented those with grocery store provisions including dried milk, dried soup, instant hot cereal, raisins, nuts, spices, strawberry jam, brown sugar, coffee and tea.

By anticipating how many days it would take me to walk between various points on the trail, I identified three small towns along the trail that could be used as pickup points for packages of food. I packed a box of food staples for each of those three towns and mailed them to myself in those towns, care of general delivery. I could further supplement my supplies at grocery stores along the way. I felt so organized!

In addition to these staples, I stuffed my backpack with brandy, clothing, my tent, my sleeping bag, a small cook stove (it wasn't that small—it weighed five pounds), fuel for the stove, pans, dishes, books, a harmonica, a hatchet (also five pounds) and other miscellaneous gear. I mailed my remaining clothing ahead to my sister in Chapel Hill.

*****

That was it! The next day, I began my great trek. I woke up early, ate breakfast, threw on my backpack and hitchhiked on State Highway 302 out of Portland. Eighty miles later, where the Appalachian Trail intersects with the highway, my ride left me off. It was two in the afternoon on a hot sunny day when I walked across the highway, following a clearly marked path into the forest.

As I began the hike, I reflected on how much I had organized in such a short time. I was pleased with how well things were going.

My path quickly turned into a steep ascent. The heat of the day seemed to increase and I became aware that my backpack was heavy. It probably weighed more than sixty-five pounds. I began to realize that I was not in hiking shape; that the amount I was carrying was much more than an experienced hiker would carry.

The steep ascent did not relent. At points along the trail, I had to pull myself up the path by grabbing onto the bases of bushes. I began to wear out. Things were not going well. I remember stopping at one point, taking off my backpack and actually beginning to cry. However, that moment of frustration quickly passed. I put on my backpack and returned to the climb.

*****

I arrived at a campsite around five that evening. It was an open area surrounded by large pines and there were no other campers. A path led from the campsite to a mountain stream which cascaded into a nearby natural pool. It had been carved by rushing water into solid rock and was about fifteen feet wide and four foot deep.

Now, I'm a person who tip-toes into a swimming pool slowly, inch by inch, taking at least ten minutes to get wet above my waist. However, after the difficult climb, the ice-cold water was the perfect medicine. I threw off my backpack, stripped naked, and jumped into the ice-cold water. It was exhilarating. At that moment, nothing I could imagine would have felt better. Fifteen minutes later, freezing but elated, I stepped out of the rock pool, got dressed and proceeded to set up my tent and fix dinner.

*****

At times, a situation which seems to be terrible during one hour can turn out to be wonderful in the next.

After setting up my tent; savoring a glass of brandy and ice water; then preparing and eating a dinner of rice cooked with a dry lentil soup mix, I felt wonderful. Confidence had returned that the trip was going to be a success! All my planning was paying off and my life was moving forward. I would complete the entire trail.

Or so I thought that evening.

*****

When I awoke the next morning, I was ready for anything that might come my way. I boiled water on my camp stove for coffee and hot cereal. Minutes later, after filling my cup with coffee, I added some brandy and put raisins and brown sugar into my hot cereal. I enjoyed that wonderful breakfast.

A half an hour later, I was back on the trail. After passing through a wooded area, the trail emerged onto a flat plane that straddled a ridge at the top of the White Mountains. The path was surrounded on both sides by delicate low-growth vegetation. My walk through that foggy morning was eerily silent—the only sounds I was able to hear being my own footsteps. I may have been on a mountain's ridge, but I was walking through a cloud; there was no view. But as the morning progressed, that cloud began to thin and I saw glimpses of distant forests and valleys on both sides.

It was peaceful. No one else was on the trail. I understood why some people prefer to hike by themselves. At one point, I left the path for a moment to scramble to the peak of a small mountain. This detour took less than five minutes. I took in the view, then returned to the path. But as I descended, it occurred to me that it takes all kinds to make a world. Some people travel long distances to conquer a mountain. I was not one of them. If the peak had been steeper or if it had required a longer detour, I wouldn't have cared to climb it. But that day, it took just a few minutes and I had climbed my first mountain peak—another notch in my belt of life!

*****

I hiked about eight miles that day and encountered only five or six other backpackers. As I labored through the day, it became clear that my backpack was too heavy and I had to lighten my load. That was accomplished by giving away extraneous foods and equipment—including my five-pound hatchet—to other hikers along the way.

That night I camped in a shed constructed on a wooden platform on the side of a forested mountain slope. The shed was sixteen feet wide and eight feet deep. It had three walls and a roof and its platform extended eight feet beyond the shed. It overlooked the mountainside and created a wonderful porch upon which I could sit gazing out across the territorial view of a forested valley. After dinner of brown rice cooked in a dried chicken soup mix, I sat on the edge of the platform with a cup of brandy. I played my harmonica that evening while watching the sunlight fade away from the hills and forests of New Hampshire.

That night, it rained. But I was comfortable, protected from the rain by the shed and my warm down sleeping bag. At dawn, the rain let up. For breakfast, I had hot coffee (with brandy), wholewheat pancakes and strawberry jelly. I also prepared a pancake and jelly sandwich for my lunch.

The rain started shortly after I hit the trail. My rain poncho fit nicely over my back pack. It rained the whole day and I ran into few hikers. I have never had a problem with being by myself and enjoyed hiking on that beautiful trail, insulated from the modern world by the sounds of rain falling and the gurgling of nearby mountain streams.

*****

I was pleased to find another shed before sunset. It was about seven miles beyond the previous night's encampment. Like the prior shelter, it had been built on a platform on the side of a hill. The shed and its open porch overlooked a wooded glen that had a stream running through it. However, I was not alone. There were already four campers there. They were all about my age. They had already eaten. So, I fixed myself a quick supper and went to sleep.

*****

I awoke the next morning to a steady rain. I spent the morning drinking coffee with my four shed-mates. Two of the campers, Jan and her boyfriend Treat, had been at the site for a couple of days. Jan was fit, confident and attractive. She and Treat both wore black and red plaid wool shirts. They got along very well. The three of us single guys were envious of Treat, a tall confident guy who obviously was quite happy to be with Jan.

As a child, Jan had lived in India where she had learned to cook. When she discovered that my food supplies included curry powder, raisins, coconut and rice, she offered to cook us all an Indian meal. We would pool our food resources for a grand feast! The rest of us were thrilled with her suggestion. That afternoon, as we sat in the shed watching the rain and sharing stories, Jan used multiple cook stoves to cook a spectacular Indian meal. She was the chef. We were her crew. And we followed her every direction without complaint.

When the various exotic dishes were close to completion, Jan sent Treat down to the creek to fill an empty wine bottle with water. (They had drunk the bottle's original contents before we arrived). Treat brought the bottle back to us full of creek water. Jan proclaimed, "Valpolicella—Wine of the gods!"

We gorged ourselves on an amazing dinner that evening. During the meal, the Valpolicella bottle was refilled with creek water multiple times. It wasn't until many years later that I learned that Valpolicella is not a white wine. It is a red wine. In the intervening years, I've drunk many different vintages of Valpolicella. But none tasted as good as that fine Valpolicella we shared that night in the White Mountains of New Hampshire.

*****

The next morning, we awoke to mist. But there was no rain. Shortly after getting up, drinking my coffee and eating my hot oatmeal, brown sugar and raisins, I was back on the trail. I had enjoyed being with others for a couple of days. But now, it felt good to be alone. Even though the rain had stopped, the underbrush was soaked and the forest was filled with the sound of water dripping from trees and bushes. That delicate, almost musical sound, blended into the gurgling of creeks, small waterfalls and rivulets.

At the end of that day, after setting up my campsite and beginning to cook dinner, I found myself missing the magic of the companions with whom I had shared an Indian meal. It occurred to me that spending a couple of months alone on the Appalachian Trail night not be as easy as I had anticipated.

The following morning, as I lathered strawberry jam onto my whole wheat pancakes, I began to question my plan to hike all the way to Georgia. What was more important—to hike the trail and see the beauty of nature; or to move forward immediately and begin creating the life that I had not succeeded in creating in Portland?

As I packed my gear into my backpack and got back onto the trail, I pondered that question and whether I should end my hike. I heard the sound of cars and trucks motoring west of me on a small highway down in a valley. I knew that catching a ride on that highway could be a means for moving forward into my future. Maybe, I could hitchhike to visit my dad in New Paltz New York, then head on down to North Carolina? About midday, I decided that even though I had enjoyed the Appalachian Trail, it was time to end the hike.

I looked at my trail map. It would take several days to get to the Appalachian Trail's next intersection with a highway. I didn't want to wait that long. I could hear vehicle traffic on the highway down in the valley. It looked like the approach to that road could be navigated. So, I decided to create my own path down the slope.

*****

Bad idea. I didn't realize what a steep jungle-like slope I had taken on. It took more than an hour of struggling without a path to descend—at times going almost vertically—to the road. I was forced to pick my way through heavy vegetation including thorny blackberries, thick bushes, fallen trees and mountain streams. When I finally arrived at the road, I was scratched, sweaty and exhausted.

In retrospect, I was quite fortunate. If I had been seriously hurt as I worked my way down to the highway, nobody would have found me. I had written to my family to tell them I planned to stay on the trail for a couple of months. If I had been seriously injured, no one would have known.

I had abandoned my Appalachian Trail plan. The food supplies I had mailed ahead to myself were never collected. But—and this was what was important—I was alive and excited to move ahead with my life.

*****

The highway to which I had found my way was a narrow two-lane road in a densely forested area. I knew that in backcountry areas, almost all traffic is local and oftentimes locals don't like outsiders. While I was relieved to have survived the thick wet underbrush of the steep slope, I was concerned as to how long it would take to catch a ride. It seemed likely that I wouldn't make it to my dad's home that night. I hoped I could at least get to a main thoroughfare so that I could get to my father's house the following day.

I waited by that road. There was almost no traffic. It took an hour and a half before I got a ride. He was driving an old Volkswagen bus that was brightly painted in paisley patterns.

The driver's name was Paul. He was a short, wiry guy, with long hair and a beard. Paul and his wife lived in Virginia. Before that, they had lived for years on acreage they still owned in Vermont. Paul's wife had just given birth to twins. He was going back to their Vermont property to retrieve some belongings.

Paul asked if I wanted to spend the night at their property—about fifty miles away from where he picked me up. The next morning, he was returning to Virginia and could leave me off next to the interstate highway. From there, I could hitchhike west across Massachusetts into New York State; then go south to visit my dad in New Paltz.

I gladly accepted Paul's offer.

Within a few hours, we arrived at Paul's property, ten mostly wooded acres. He parked his Volkswagen van in the middle of a clearing surrounded by a forest of large hardwood trees. In the center of the clearing was a huge oak. About fifteen feet up it was a treehouse with a rope ladder descending from it. Paul told me I could sleep in the treehouse. He would sleep in the van.

That sounded good.

It was supper time. Paul started a fire in a large pit and prepared an excellent lentil soup. After dinner, we sat around the fire and talked. He told me how much he loved his wife; how excited they were to have twins—two baby girls! I told him about my hike on the Appalachian Trail; about my plans for the future.

*****

After the sun set, we watched the fire burn down. Paul pulled out a small metal pipe and put some hashish in it. He lit the hashish and took a drag. Then he passed the pipe to me. I took a couple of drags. I had smoked hash a couple of times before. But this stuff was really powerful. I was seriously stoned.

We sat staring at the fire. Paul began to talk about his philosophy of life. More than once, he referenced his favorite book, *Stranger in a Strange Land*. I had read the book and enjoyed it. But I also was aware that it had been the murderer Charles Manson's favorite book. I started to become a little worried—then afraid. Paul looked an awful lot like Charles Manson. I started to panic. How did I know that this guy who said his name was Paul really had a wife—

or any new babies? How did I know anything he had told me was the truth? Did I need to get out of there?

I told Paul I was tired and wanted to turn in. He replied, "Great. I'm tired too."

I climbed up into the treehouse and carefully latched the trap door on the treehouse floor. I rolled out my sleeping bag and tried to go to sleep. But I lay there worrying for quite a while. Finally, I fell asleep.

*****

I awoke early the next morning no longer stoned and not paranoid any longer. The only sounds I could hear were birds in the trees. I looked out of the treehouse's small window and saw Paul cooking over the campfire. I rolled up my sleeping bag, gathered my belongings and climbed down from the treehouse.

Paul was fixing a kettle of steel cut oats over the fire. I watched him cut up dried apricots and stir them into a steaming pot of cereal. He handed me a blue enamel metal cup, then picked up the blue enamel coffee pot sitting next to the fire and poured me a cup of strong, very good coffee.

As I drank the coffee, Paul asked, "Did you sleep well?"

I said, "Yes, I did. I was pretty paranoid last night."

"Yeah," he laughed. "I noticed that. That was some pretty powerful hash and you had already had an intense day. I wasn't too surprised. You needed a good night's rest and it looks like you got it."

Then Paul served me steel cut oats in a blue enamel metal bowl. A lot of how something tastes is driven by the circumstances in which you eat it. Here I was, sitting in front of a fire in the midst of a forest of gigantic oaks having just had a great night's sleep. Life was good. I had a lot to be thankful for—and I was eating the best hot cereal I'd ever tasted.

After breakfast, Paul washed the dishes. Then we packed up the van and were on our way. Paul had come through on everything he offered. He shared his food and his treehouse. Then he gave me a ride to Interstate 90 in Massachusetts.

Sometimes, people are extremely generous and ask for nothing in return. Now, many years later, I feel indebted to Paul for his generosity and kind spirit. I hope Paul, his wife and their daughters are enjoying a good life.

*****

Before leaving Portland, I had written my dad to let him know I was hiking the Appalachian Trail. There was no way he or Sally could have anticipated that I would show up at their home that day. I stopped at a pay phone and called to let them know I was coming. A few hours later, I was welcomed into their home and warmly encouraged to stay as long as I wanted. I was there for a little more than a week. It was a great visit. But I wanted to get on with my life's adventures.

When I was ready to leave New Paltz, my dad and Sally insisted on driving me down to North Carolina.

*****

All families are complicated. When parents divorce, family politics make it even worse. My mother's anger had caused her to create a rift between my father and me. My father's busy schedule had easily accommodated that rift. I had avoided getting to know Sally. But that was history now. My father and I were communicating. I was beginning to get to know Sally. Those few days I spent in New Paltz were wonderful.

After driving me to Chapel Hill, North Carolina, my father and Sally stayed an additional day at my sister Diane's home to celebrate my 22nd birthday. After they departed for New Paltz, I sat down on a chair in Diane's living room and broke down crying. I told Diane it was so wonderful having my father back.

Diane and I have always been very close. Our parents' divorce secured that bond. Now, she was thrilled that I had chosen to live near her. She and her husband Richard lived in an old, very small and sweet, one-bedroom house.

It was the beginning of October, 1971. I needed to figure out what would be next in my life—and then make it happen.

5—Greensboro

The University of North Carolina is located in Chapel Hill. Duke University is just a few miles away in Durham. My brother-in-law was getting a master's degree in Greek and Roman Classical Literature. My sister was teaching photography at a Chapel Hill free university. They each had good reasons to live in a college town. I didn't.

After four long years as a college student, I felt no affection towards what I considered to be the arrogant and unreal world of students. Theoretical radicalism—talking big and doing nothing—made my ass tired. Nor was I impressed by the working-class costumes that students wore to impress one other. So, if you hadn't already guessed, I considered college communities to be pretentious and lacking perspective. I wanted a real job doing real work in a real community.

The morning after my dad and Sally returned to New York, I asked Diane for a suggestion of where I should live. I was impatient to get on with my life. I told her I wanted to be nearby, but didn't want to live in Chapel Hill. She understood and suggested Greensboro, a working-class town of one hundred and forty thousand residents located about fifty miles west of Chapel Hill. While Greensboro did have a public college, the city wasn't dominated by students.

*****

A couple of days later, I borrowed my sister's 1954 Volkswagen (a car already qualifying as a collector's item) and drove to Greensboro. I began my exploration of the city at a shopping area near the college campus. Even though I didn't want to be connected to the college, students and others who lived in that area would be able to give me some

perspective on what it would be like to live in Greensboro—
and on how hard it would be to find a job.

I've often been lucky in finding the right thing at the
right time. Sometimes, it has been almost uncanny how
what I am looking for seemingly jumps into my lap.

I parked in front of a Christian bookstore. Though I
am as culturally and religiously un-Christian as you will
find, for some reason I went into the Christian bookstore to
ask for advice about jobs and housing. The shopkeeper was
young and friendly. I told her a little about myself and asked
how hard she thought it would be to find a job and a
moderately priced apartment in Greensboro. In a gentle
voice with a sweet North Carolinian accent, she told me she
had a friend who lived in a centrally located medium-sized
apartment building. Most of its tenants were young and she
believe their rent was modest.

I wrote down the apartment's address, then asked
about the job scene.

"What sort of job are you looking for?"

"I'm looking for some sort of manual labor."

"Would you, for example, be interested in a
construction labor job?"

"Absolutely. That would be perfect."

"Well, in that case I know of one situation that you
might want to check out. My daddy owns a small
construction company. They build houses and commercial
buildings. I don't know if he has any openings right now. But
you might want to give him a call. You can tell him that I
referred you."

I was stunned. She gave me his business card. Her
father's name was Claudius Dockery III. I wasn't sure what
the *III* stood for. Later found out that his dad and

grandfather had been important public figures in Greensboro's history.

I gave her a big thank you and was on my way.

*****

I called Mr. Dockery about an hour later. The moment he answered the phone, I knew where his daughter had gotten her accent.

"Mr. Dockery, I am looking for a job. Your daughter gave me your name. I'm a hard worker and wondered if you might have any manual labor jobs."

In a gentle, but firm, manner, Dockery replied. "I'm not certain if I will be able to be of any help. But, out of respect for my daughter, I would be pleased to meet with you."

We agreed to meet at his office the following day.

I headed over to the apartment complex. It was a U-shaped, single-story building with thirty units. I called the phone number shown on the *Units for Rent* sign. An hour later, I was met by someone who showed me an apartment. The unfurnished unit had a living room, bedroom, bathroom and small kitchen. The monthly rent was seventy dollars plus first and last months' rent. If I took the apartment, I'd have to sign a twelve-month lease.

I told the leasing agent that I would get back to him in a couple days.

*****

The following day, I drove back to Greensboro for my interview with Mr. Dockery. Dockery was a carefully groomed man. He wore a beige three-piece suit, white shirt and tie and sported a medium length, perfectly cut, perfectly combed hairdo—there was not a single hair out of place. Mr.

56

Dockery was businesslike, but gracious, in asking about my work experience.

I told him I was a hard worker and not afraid of physical work. But I was honest. I had no on-the-job construction experience.

Dockery asked the question I would be asked many times over the next few years. "Why would anyone with a college education want to earn low wages doing back breaking work?"

"I always have enjoyed physical labor. I like being outside and I don't want to work in an office."

"How did you meet my daughter?"

"I just walked into her shop."

Being straightforward with Mr. Dockery had been the right approach.

"Well, Roger—I am willing to give you a try. The work is hard. I expect you to fit in and be a constructive part of Dockery Lumber Company. If it isn't working out in about a week, I will ask you to leave. The job pays two dollars an hour. But Roger, I want you to cut your hair and shave off your mustache."

I wasn't surprised by that request. It was 1971. I was in North Carolina. The United States was involved in the war in Viet Nam and young people with long hair and moustaches or beards were viewed as trouble-makers. While change might have been coming, even to the South, it wasn't welcomed by everyone. My hair was shoulder length and I had a fairly long, if somewhat stringy, mustache. I don't think Dockery had a personal issue with my hair or mustache. He just didn't want conflict among his employees.

"Would it be sufficient," I asked, "if I just cut off my mustache and stuffed my hair up inside my hardhat?"

"That might work, Roger. I'll give it a try. But if it appears it isn't working out, I'll ask you to cut your hair."

We shook hands and had a deal. I would start the following Monday.

*****

Then, I drove to the office of the apartment management company, paid my first and last month's rent, signed a one-year lease and got the keys to my new apartment.

But I wasn't done for the day. I went to the Salvation Army store which was only a couple of blocks from my new apartment. I bought a broken couch, a used mattress, a lamp and some assorted cooking and dining gear. The couch only had three legs. But I figured I would be able to figure out how to add a fourth.

I guess I was feeling inspired. My new apartment was about four miles from Dockery Lumber Company. I went into a Schwinn bicycle store and, for a hundred dollars, bought a new yellow ten-speed bicycle. I would ride my bicycle to and from work each day. The money I saved by not having to pay bus fare would easily pay for the bike. Smart thinking, Roger!

When I returned to my sister's home that evening, I felt supremely successful. I had been hired as a construction worker with a company that was large enough to give me opportunities to advance and small enough to be personal. I had an apartment, had already partially furnished it and had purchased a bike. My life was on a roll.

The next day, I returned to Greensboro by bus and moved into my new apartment.

*****

The following Monday morning was dark and rainy, I rode my bike into work. I arrived on time, but the bike ride had worn me out—before I'd even begun my workday! That was the only time I rode my bike into work. From that point forward, I took the city bus.

On that first day, I was assigned to go out on a job with a supervisor named Bobby Wyrick. We installed a vapor seal on a home that had been constructed around 1900. As we crouched on our hands and knees, rolling out plastic sheets across the crawl space under the house, Bobby told me about himself. He had worked for Dockery Lumber for decades. But his family's history in the Greensboro area went much further back. His great-grandfather had been a plantation owner. He had owned slaves.

Bobby told me in his slow North Carolina accent, "Before the Civil War, things were better for everyone, including the Negros. Then, the carpet baggers from the North came down. They destroyed what had been a beautiful way of life—for everyone."

I was smart enough to listen and not share any of my opinions. I asked questions about life for the slaves that required Bobby to think a little before he responded. But I was respectful. Bobby Wyrick had a lot of affection for a time and a way of life that had predated his birth by over seventy years.

*****

I have learned that showing respect for others is the most important skill to bring into any new environment. Too many people come into a new situation and immediately judge it based upon their own experiences. They often arrive at conclusions about people before they understand them. In so doing, they announce their own arrogance. I was humble enough not to make that stupid error. One of the benefits of listening first was that those I met set aside some of their assumptions about me. They gave me a chance.

The other benefit of listening was that I learned from and about others. There are very few situations or places where you cannot learn something from the people whom you meet.

Mr. Dockery probably had me spend that first day with Bobby Wyrick to give Bobby a chance to size me up— was I capable of being a team player instead of a distraction? I think I passed the test. I worked hard and I listened. I think that was what Dockery wanted.

*****

Bobby Wyrick and I probably took about seven or eight cigarette breaks during that first day of work at Dockery Lumber. Cigarettes were a very important part of the North Carolinian culture. You smoked when you talked. You smoked after you ate. And you smoked during coffee breaks. I enjoyed the breaks, the coffee and even the cigarettes. Many of the people I worked with in Greensboro are probably dead now, a lot of them killed by cancer caused by those cigarettes that they enjoyed so much. One of the blessings of my life is that I never got hooked on cigarettes.

*****

The next day I broke down and spent the twenty cents (each way) to take the city bus into work. It was quicker and definitely required less effort. That second day, I worked with two other laborers, Shorty and Archie. We dug a ditch. Shorty had been with the company forever. He was about 60-years-old and had worked for Claudius

Dockery II before working for his son. Shorty did not work hard. But he talked a lot. And oh, by the way, Shorty wasn't too tall.

Archie was also around sixty. In addition to being a highly skilled cement mason, Archie was an intelligent and considerate person. I had the pleasure of working with Archie on a number of projects during my time at Dockery Lumber. He was the highest-paid black employee at the company and knew more about working with cement, stucco and mortar than anyone else at the company. However, because Archie was black, his title was *laborer*. A white skilled craftsman would not have been sent out to dig a ditch on a slow day. However, that was the double standard that existed in North Carolina in 1971.

Archie, Shorty and I worked on our ditch. I went at it with a vigor that was not appreciated by Shorty. He seemed to take a cigarette break after each shovelful of soil. Finally, Shorty said to me, "You know, Roger. The ditch isn't going anywhere. It'll still be here in the afternoon."

That was another lesson. If you are new and if you work harder than your co-workers, it pisses them off. That being said, kicking back because your co-workers are screwing off all of the time is also problematic. I never fully figured out the resolution to that dilemma.

*****

Each workday morning, most Dockery Lumber workers congregated at the company's offices. New crew assignments and project changes were announced at that time. Then, at a little before eight, crews piled into pickup trucks and headed out to jobsites to begin their day's work.

On my third morning with the company, as I stood waiting, hard hat and lunch pail in hand, Mr. Dockery walked up to me and said, "Roger, today you'll be working on Rudy's bricklaying crew. You're going to be a brick tender and are being assigned to Rudy on an ongoing basis. If you like the work, you might eventually get to be an apprentice. Then someday, you might become a journeyman bricklayer. We'll just see how it goes."

That day, I learned that brick tenders assist journeyman bricklayers by delivering bricks and mortar, setting up and taking down scaffolding, and generally doing whatever lower-level work helps bricklayers use their time most effectively.

*****

My experience at Dockery Lumber was to be largely defined by the crew to which I was now assigned. The crew was a reflection of its foreman, Rudy. Rudy had a college education—but didn't advertise that fact. He spoke directly to us, letting each of us know in no uncertain terms when he wasn't pleased with how the work was getting done. But that sort of communication was rarely required. Rudy laid brick alongside the rest of the crew and was immensely respected by each of us. Under his leadership, we had a lot of fun, were highly productive and produced quality work.

Ed Lemmons, a brick mason, was a sixty-year-old, down-home, good old boy. Ed was humble and quiet in demeanor. To describe Ed, but not describe his son Roger at the same time, was to miss a lot of Ed's personality. Roger, also a bricklayer, was about thirty. Like his father, he was a good old boy. But Roger was a *big* good old boy. Roger must have weighed almost three hundred pounds. Ed and Roger were both deeply Christian, loved hunting, home cooked foods, stock-car racing and America.

Dennis was the final bricklayer on our crew. He was from Richmond Virginia where his wife and kids still lived, but where the construction industry had become depressed. Dennis didn't talk a lot. When he did speak, he liked to tell us about sleeping with young women with big breasts.

Steve was an apprentice. But his duties were identical to mine. He was nineteen years old and really loved girls. In addition to his fiancé, Steve had several girlfriends. He had a great sense of humor and often patiently explained to me nuances of the culture of North Carolina.

Pete mixed the mortar for the crew. He was a black man in his mid-fifties. Pete was overweight, very soft spoken and always deferred to others on the crew. Pete had been raised in the backwoods and had a large family, but spoke only rarely of them. I only remember one personal story Pete shared. It was about a possum he had trapped. Pete explained to me that possum are dirty animals. They eat garbage, feed off of carrion and prey upon other small animals. Pete told me he'd trapped a possum that summer and had caged the animal for several months; feeding it cornmeal and other grains to clean out its system; fattening it up before he butchered it. Pete said that that possum would be the best Thanksgiving dinner his family had ever had.

*****

The biggest part of what Steve and I did was deliver bricks to the bricklayers. That meant loading wheelbarrows full of bricks, then wheeling them over to, and stacking them for, each mason. All of this was intense backbreaking work.

Laying brick for facia on a two or three-story building required pitching bricks up onto scaffolding. Steve or I would pitch bricks; the other would catch and stack them neatly on the scaffold next to each bricklayer. We pitched two, three, and sometimes four bricks at a time. On three-story buildings, we had to send them up to an intermediate point, then repeat the effort a second time to get them all the way up to the masons.

Moving mortar to masons on the scaffolding meant that one of us removed mortar from Pete's wheelbarrow, one shovelful at a time, and handed that loaded shovel up to the other on the scaffolding. We transferred the mortar from mortar board to mortar board, up the scaffolding, until each mason had sufficient mortar on their mortar board.

Rudy, Dennis, Ed and Roger were superb bricklayers. Steve, Pete and I knew how to hustle. We each took a great deal of pride in the quality of our work. Other Dockery Lumber crews treated us with respect. When our backlog of work grew, it wasn't because we had slowed down. It was because we'd been assigned more of the company's largest and most complex jobs.

*****

My first day as a brick tender was physically painful. As the day progressed, my hands started to bleed from handling brick. Steve took me aside and gave me a pair of thick rubber gloves. He explained that the bricks would eventually create calluses on my hands. But until those calluses were created, my hands were going to be destroyed if I didn't wear protective gloves. He recommended I buy another two or three pair.

I came home from work that first night in total pain. Every muscle in my body spoke to me loudly. My hands were red, sore and still bleeding. I took a hot bath, fixed a dinner of canned corn beef hash with fried eggs and went to bed. I slept until it was time to go to work the following morning.

*****

After I had worked on Rudy's crew for three or four days, Mr. Dockery pulled me aside. "Roger—I asked Rudy how you were doing. He told me you're pulling your weight. So, you can consider yourself a regular employee."

He paused and added, "How do you like the job?"

"Thank you, Mr. Dockery. I like the job a lot. And Rudy and the others have been great to work with. But I think the work is worth more than two dollars an hour. I think it's worth $2.25 an hour."

Dockery said he would check with Rudy and get back to me. He never got back to me. But on my first check, I was paid at the $2.25 per hour wage.

*****

One day during our lunch break, some squirrels were scurrying in a tree above us. Steve said, "I wish I had my gun."

I said, "What for?"

Steve looked at me in disbelief and asked, "Haven't you ever eaten squirrel pie?"

"No, I haven't," I responded, "and I'm not interested in starting now."

Steve laughed. "You're crazy. Squirrel pie is about the best damn meal in the whole world."

Roger and Ed Lemmons chimed in with enthusiastic agreement.

We all laughed. Me at them—them at me.

*****

Sometimes, Rudy would yell out, "Get it, get it, get it, get it!" It wasn't a sign of disrespect and the crew wasn't offended. It was a sign that there was a lot of work to do—

that Rudy had confidence in his team. We always responded by working harder.

We would chat with one another while we worked. Ed would tell stories about brick masons he had known over the years. Roger would tell us about his favorite NASCAR driver. Steve would describe the girl he was hustling—or the one who he had a date coming up with—or a fight with his fiancé. And Dennis would tell us about the size of the breasts of the girl he'd seen at a bar the other night.

The crew argued about meaningless issues. But discussions never were personal or serious. Mutual respect among team members was the standard. And the most constant factor in all of our conversations was laughter.

*****

One day, while I was stacking bricks, the Lemmons were giving me a tough time on some meaningless issue. I didn't back down and was razzing them back, an insult for an insult. Rudy decided that the banter had gone on long enough and hollered out, "Hippy, get over here!"

From that day forward, my fate was sealed. My name at Dockery Lumber was *Hippy* or *Hip*—never Roger. I think the difference between *Hippy* and *Hip* was that *Hippy* was my formal name—sort of like *Roger* or *James*. *Hip* was more personalized—like *Rog* or *Jim*. In any case, I understood that by giving me a nickname, my co-workers had accepted me—along with any differences they might have perceived in who I was or how I acted.

Steve's last name was Whit. A couple of days after Rudy christened me "Hippy", he called Steve over. "Whip!" he said. "Get over here!" From that day forward, we were *Hip* and *Whip* to everyone at Dockery Lumber.

I kept my promise to Mr. Dockery—about shaving off my mustache. I also kept my promise about keeping my hair up in my hat—for a week or two. After the second week, when I arrived the Dockery Lumber office in the morning, I would shove my hair up under my stocking cap or hardhat. Once I was out at a jobsite, however, I let my hair hang down. It never bothered anyone. Even Mr. Dockery had seen me at worksites with my hair down. He never commented on it. But Dockery also stopped calling me *Roger* and started calling me *Hip*.

*****

Our crew couldn't lay brick when it was very rainy or cold. On those days, I was assigned to work on another crew. It was through those assignments that I got to know other workers at Dockery Lumber. When I arrived at a jobsite with a new crew, I was quizzed by the workers about my background. The typical question was: "Why in the hell are you out here working on a construction job when you got a college education?"

I was an oddity. But that was ok. I wanted to earn their respect.

One day, I was digging a trench for a foundation's footing. A young laborer from a framing crew walked up to me and said, "Ok. Let's wrestle."

I had no clue where he was coming from or if he was serious. We'd never had a conflict. I knew it wasn't a good thing to fight on the job, but when he grabbed me and started throwing me to the ground, I had no choice. This young laborer had seriously underestimated my strength. I was pretty tall and skinny, but I was also fairly strong. It took me about a minute to pin him in a large square footing hole. After about thirty seconds, he informed me we could stop wrestling—which I did with relief.

The wrestling match was over. I will never know what prompted it. But he and I became buddies—and the rest of his crew treated me as if I had been initiated.

Such is life.

*****

One rainy day, I was sent out to install a curtain drain in the back yard of a completed home. A supervisor named John took me out to the jobsite. John was about sixty years old. He had short blond curly hair and a blonde carefully trimmed mustache. Instead of smoking a cigarette, he puffed on a pipe and had a friendly, easy-going demeanor. We chatted as we rode in his pickup. John told me about his background. He had a college degree and had worked in multiple countries and diverse industries before coming to North Carolina. He shared his perspectives on working at Dockery Lumber Company. After hearing his thoughts about the culture at Dockery, I realized John understood a whole lot more about the people we worked with than he let on to others.

John told me a joke that was typical of his easy style. To this day, it is one of my favorites.

Every October, three doctors—Bob and his two friends—took a two-week moose hunting trip. They stayed deep in the woods at an old, but comfortable, hunting lodge. Over the years they'd eaten eat well on their trips, rotating cooking responsibilities on a daily basis.

In this particular year, one of Bob's friends suggested a change in how kitchen duties would be assigned. One of the three would cook until the others complained. Then meal preparation duties would go to a second person who would cook until the others bitched about the meals. In that way, kitchen responsibilities would rotate between the three friends for the entire trip.

The three doctors drew straws to see who would cook first. Bob drew the short straw. He didn't mind. The cabin had a nicely equipped, well stocked kitchen and he enjoyed cooking. Also, he'd been working hard at his clinic prior to the trip and taking a few days to relax in the kitchen seemed like a nice break.

However, after six or seven days of preparing meals, Bob realized that the other two had set him up. They weren't going to complain about anything he fixed. It made no difference what he prepared; his friends were going to say they liked it.

Bob realized that drastic action was necessary if he didn't want to cook for the entire trip. That evening, he fixed prime rib, baked potatoes and green beans with slivered almonds. For dessert, he baked a pie crust. Then, he walked into the woods searching for the right size of moose crap. He found one and brought it back to the kitchen, placing it in the baked pie shell.

That night, Bob's friends went heavy on the praise telling him, "Great meal Bob. You cook better than the wife!" and "You're spoiling us, Bob."

Bob ignored the teasing. After clearing dinner plates, he brought out the pie and cut a large piece for each of his buddies. His friend who took the first big bite of pie shuddered and shouted, "Moose shit pie!" But then added, "But good!"

*****

While John told me the joke, his eyes focused on the road ahead. But he turned to me with a wry smile as he said, "But good!"

That joke is typical of the good spirited fun that went on between employees at Dockery. To this day, I use the phrase "Moose shit pie, but good!" to laugh away something unpleasant.

*****

John and I arrived at the jobsite—a nice suburban residence. He showed me the spot in the backyard where water pooled whenever it rained; then seeped into the home's family room.

John said, "We need to put in a curtain drain. Dig a ditch around the patio and fill it with several inches of gravel. Then, put perforated drainage pipe along the entire ditch. Once you've done that, cover the pipe with tarpaper and gravel; then cover it all with topsoil."

"In order for the curtain drain to function properly," he added, "the drainage pipe has to get progressively deeper. The gradual slope will allow rainwater to flow from the beginning of the curtain drain to its end and away from the house."

John asked if I understood. I did. He told me he had to go to another jobsite and would pick me up at the end of the workday.

I said, "What do I do if I finish before you return?

He smiled and said, "You can go home".

When he returned that afternoon to pick me up, I was gone. My shovel was laying on the ground, broken in half. But the curtain drain had been completed.

A couple of weeks later, John took me aside. "The other day, I said you could go home after you were done because I knew putting in that sort of curtain drain is a two-day job. Curtain drains often fail because they are not properly installed. The homeowners called me yesterday. They're thrilled with how well the curtain drain is working. Good job, Hip."

A compliment like that meant a lot to me.

*****

In Greensboro, I established a variety of regular personal routines. Before going to work, I got up at six and fixed coffee and a plate of fried eggs, bacon and toast. After breakfast, I packed my lunch—a couple of packaged deli meat sandwiches, two oatmeal marshmallow-filled sandwich cookies and a thermos of coffee. Then, I was off to catch the city bus.

On Saturdays, I pedaled my bike around town, did my grocery shopping, washed my clothes and straightened up my apartment. Then I pedaled to the Hostess Bakery Outlet Store and purchased whole wheat bread for sandwiches and marshmallow-filled cookies.

Sundays were special. I've always been a big sports fan. I'd find a way to watch professional football on Sunday afternoons even when I didn't have a TV or radio. In Greensboro, I found a student television lounge at the local college where I watched the NFL.

I was putting my world in order.

*****

I took pride in my apartment. When I moved in, the living room was painted dark tan. I decided the room needed a little color. One Saturday morning in late October, I bought a gallon of Sears' cheapest rose-beige indoor paint and started rolling the paint onto my living room walls. It didn't take long to realize that one gallon wasn't going to finish the job. I needed more paint. So, I added water to the paint that was left. After all, it was water-based, right? Why not?

Needless to say, when I was done, the paint job didn't exactly look professional. But I was sort of impressed with the unusual effect created by the watered-down rose-beige paint over the much darker base.

I borrowed some wood working tools and made a counter for my kitchen. It looked nice! A neighbor asked if I would be willing to help him make a similar counter for his kitchen! While I don't think I ever helped my neighbor on that project, the compliment puffed up my craftsman's ego.

*****

I had no friends. More specifically and to the point, I didn't have a girlfriend.

There was a nice coffee house next to the college campus. On weekend evenings, it featured local folk singers. One Saturday evening, I visited the coffee house. I walked in the door and saw a strikingly beautiful young woman. She was over six feet tall, had long black hair and deeply shadowed eyes. The woman was wearing a dark blue scarf and long deep-red coat. I can't remember how I started chatting with her and her friends, but I was immediately enchanted with her musical North Carolinian accent. After a couple of beers, I decided that this might just turn into a real romance.

Her name was Loretta. She was from a small town in eastern North Carolina. She told me my lifestyle seemed exciting. That puffed up my confidence. Over the next couple of months, I went over to Loretta's apartment several times. I enjoyed chatting with Loretta and her friends. She seemed to like me. But her friends clearly thought I was strange. One of them always referred to me as *Roger Over and Way Out*.

*****

One Friday evening in early November, I visited a bar near my apartment. I had been there before on weekday evenings. That evening, a sign on the door advertised a blues singer's performance. That seemed cool!

I sat down at a table and ordered a drink. A few minutes later, a black woman stepped up to the microphone on a small stage. She started singing the blues. The woman was large—not fat—and had long black thickly curled hair and very dark skin. Her voice was rich and she sang with passion. One song she sang in a haunting manner was entitled, *When there is something wrong with my baby, there is something wrong with me*. If I close my eyes right now, I can still hear her rich rendition of that song.

Since my first evening at the coffee house with Loretta, our relationship hadn't been moving forward much—but not for lack of effort on my part. When I heard the blues singer, I realized that asking Loretta out and taking her to hear her sing would be the perfect date!

I asked Loretta—did she want to go? She responded with an enthusiastic *yes*.

On the following Saturday evening, Loretta and I went to the night club to hear my blues singer. It was a full house. We got a center table near the stage. When the vocalist came out to sing, her voice was just as deep, strong and soulful as I remembered. Loretta was impressed. I was feeling pretty good. However, soon the performance changed from what I had seen the previous week. On her third song, the blues singer took off her blouse. I was embarrassed. I explained to Loretta that she hadn't done that the first time I had heard her sing. Loretta didn't say a lot. Our date ended early.

*****

Around the time I met Loretta, I met a guy from Washington DC named Mike. Mike and I had a couple of things in common. We had both recently graduated from college and we were both trying to make a life for ourselves in Greensboro, North Carolina.

Mike had originally stayed in DC after graduating. But he met a young woman who was visiting his friends. They dated. When the woman returned to her home in Greensboro, Mike followed her and moved in with her. Mike was head over heels in love.

Having a friend was a big deal for me. Mike and I got together about once a week for a beer or dinner. I met Mike's girlfriend Becky. She was originally from Winston Salem, a nearby city. Her father was a preacher. Becky was as cute as Mike had promised. She paid no attention to me and my impression of her was that she just wasn't hip.

*****

I also met Becky's roommate Ellie. Ellie loved to laugh and had a brilliant, but sarcastic, sense of humor. I got together with Ellie and her sister Sarah several times. We had fun and laughed a lot. They called me *Rogers*. I didn't know the significance of adding an *s* onto my name. But I didn't mind. I was so pleased to have more friends.

One Saturday morning, Ellie and Sarah invited me to join them on a jewelry store expedition. We would be looking at diamonds. Ellie and Sarah knew more about diamonds than I ever will. Their family had descended from North Carolinian gentry and their confident demeanor impressed the jewelers. The jewelry saleswoman pulled out the store's biggest jewels and let us look at them through a microscope. It was silly, fascinating and fun. That was typical of the whimsical sort of play I enjoyed with these sisters.

*****

I mention these relationships because when you're living by yourself, in a place where you know no one else, small friendships mean a whole lot. It wasn't that I was lonely. I always found things to do that were absolutely fascinating. But, spending time with a person who knew who I was, and who would speak with me—well—that was really nice.

I was developing skills in my job. I had some friends. I had met a woman with whom I was trying to establish a relationship. I watched football on Sundays and occasionally went to a bar.

Life was becoming full!

*****

At work, I was getting along fine with my co-workers. The first step in earning respect from others is to demonstrate respect for them. God knows that the people I worked with expected a northerner with a college education to be an arrogant know-it-all. My co-workers recognized that my life had been different than theirs. But I think they ended up enjoying the differences. I certainly enjoyed seeing, hearing and learning about their lives. Every day at work was unique and introduced me to things that were totally new.

*****

One week, our crew made structural repairs to a house that had been constructed in the 1840s. The home had a brick foundation; its bricks handcrafted by slaves.

Handling those bricks touched me—holding something in my hands that had been created under such painful conditions—well it was humbling.

The nuances of that worksite were compounded. Archie, a black man, was repairing the house's old-fashioned masonry fireplace. His knowledge and skills allowed him to make many repairs for which no one else at Dockery Lumber Company had the skills. In retrospect, the degree to which white people, who did not look up to black people, depended on them—well, it's worth being aware of.

*****

At work, black and white folks treated one another respectfully. No reference was ever made to a person's color. But on an ongoing basis, there was a clear and consistent deferral by black employees to white employees—a behavior fully expected by the white employees.

Each day, our crew sat down on a square of bricks or stack of lumber to eat lunch. Sometimes we ate quietly. Other times we chatted briskly. However, Pete always sat and ate his lunch about fifteen or twenty feet away from the rest of the crew, waiting to be included in a conversation before participating. No rules were written or spoken. No admonitions given. That's just how it was.

One day, after I'd been on the crew for several months, I asked Pete to come on over and sit by the rest of us. There was a large and awkward silence. Everyone felt uncomfortable for a moment. But after no one objected, Pete shrugged his shoulders, slowly walked over and sat down to eat his lunch next to the others. From that day forward, Pete sat and ate with the rest of the crew.

I guess that may have been a change that was ready to happen. It just needed the door to be pushed open a little bit. Sometimes, your responsibility for change is to push on a door. Sometimes, you shouldn't depend upon others to announce that the time is right.

*****

Working with my crew was fun. I'd never had a job which combined such hard work with so much laughter.

One time, Roger Lemmons was explaining to me that North Carolina is really a lot colder than Minnesota. Roger's actual words were: "In the winter in North Carolina, it gets so cold outside that when you talk to somebody, your words freeze before they get to the other person."

I responded, "In Minnesota, we call that spring."

That was the sort of humor we shared as we worked. It made for good laughter and helped the days pass quickly.

*****

Mike and I would get together from time to time. His girlfriend Becky was never included. During our visits, Mike would talk about how much he loved Becky—and how concerned he was that their relationship might end. We've all been there. We've all had friends who have been there. It's a bummer.

In December, Mike told me he and Becky were having problems, that Becky didn't like him so much anymore. He told me he might be moving back to DC. I chalked it up to insecurity. However, a couple days later, Mike told me he was going back to DC. He encouraged me to become friends with Becky. I hardly knew her and dismissed his suggestion. I was focused upon somehow developing my relationship with Loretta—even though I had not had a lot of success to date.

Days later, Mike moved away. I'd lost my only friend.

*****

A few days later, Becky called me asking if I wanted to go to a movie. I was surprised to hear from her. But I had been lonely and was glad to have something to do—with anyone. We went to a movie and then we talked a lot. Becky told me living in North Carolina left her feeling trapped. She said she enjoyed getting together with me because I was from a different place. She wanted to grow beyond the world in which she had been raised.

Becky and I started going to an occasional dinner and a movie. We laughed a lot. It was fun. But it definitely wasn't romantic.

*****

Dockery Lumber Company shut down operations for a week between Christmas and New Year's. During that week, I took a Greyhound Bus back to Minnesota to attend my sister's wedding. She was marrying her live-in boyfriend, Richard. When I returned from the trip, the weather had cooled. On wet and particularly cold days, I was given work with another crew or told I could take the day off. On one of those cold wet days, I was at home when I received a call from Becky. She and Ellie had had an argument. Ellie told Becky to move out of the house. Becky was wondering if she and her big dog Ducky could stay at my place for a couple days until she found another place to live.

I was loyal to Mike (and protective of myself). I told her, "Sure, but you sleep on the couch."

*****

So, Becky moved in with me and she slept on the couch—and Ducky peed all over the apartment. Becky and I enjoyed one another's company. Our friendship grew. We shared life stories, laughed a lot, continued going to films and discussing them afterwards.

Greensboro was about twenty-five miles away from Becky's hometown. Becky's father was a minister. As a southern minister, propriety was important. Becky had long since rebelled against that propriety.

Becky's parents had us over for dinner. Becky's father was not very pleased that his daughter was living with a man. It certainly didn't make things a lot better that that man was Jewish. Becky warned me her father would try to make me feel uncomfortable by not speaking to me more than absolutely necessary. That was all the warning I needed.

During the meal, I became the chattiest person you've ever met in your life. Becky's father tried to make me feel uncomfortable by refusing to speak to me. But I was not intimidated. I'd put up with pompous adults all my life. Her father was perplexed that I didn't even seem to notice his efforts to ignore me. I think her mother understood what I was doing. She'd probably seen his self-righteous act often enough and enjoyed seeing it fail. After we left, Becky and I laughed about it all the way home.

Becky and I were the same age and had graduated from college at the same time. We both were more concerned about growing as individuals than in settling down to start careers and families. We were part of a generation that was questioning the values of the communities in which we had grown up. We wanted more integrity in our lives than we had seen in the lives of our parents' generation.

*****

I still had a crush on Loretta. However, she had made it crystal clear that she was not going to become romantically involved with me. Still, she allowed me to visit her. I tried to explain that Becky's moving in was only temporary. I made it very clear that Becky and I were not involved in a love relationship—that I was just sharing my apartment with her because she was a friend in need—and only until she got her own place. Loretta wasn't buying it. She did not respond warmly. Even though she claimed to not want a relationship with me, she didn't seem to want me to have one with anyone else either.

A couple of weeks later, Becky had a bad dream in the middle of the night and wanted to tell me about it. She moved from my couch into my bedroom.

*****

Becky and I enjoyed being together. I was pleased to have a relationship. However, I was cautious and not about to fall in love. Watching my parents' unhappy marriage had instilled in me a distinct fear of anything that seemed like a real commitment.

One Sunday evening, after a day spent doing odds and ends together, Becky and I were sitting together on my living room couch. We were facing one another; our feet up on the couch; talking about how comfortable we made each other feel. Becky told me that hanging out with me was like being with a girlfriend. She didn't mean that as an insult. I think she meant that she didn't have to put on a show for me—that I was an ally.

*****

During the winter in Greensboro, construction work was not as much fun as it had been in the fall. Due to the cold and wet weather, I was only working about four days a week. When I did work, I often worked with one of the carpentry crews.

Bobby Wyrick, who worked with me on my first day on the job, had two brothers who also had worked for years as supervisors at Dockery Lumber. Their names were Billy and Jimmy. Jimmy was generally called *Chop-it-off* behind his back. But no one ever called him that to his face. I didn't know how he got the nick-name *Chop-it-off.*

One day I was assigned to work on Jimmy's carpentry crew. One of his carpenters had been installing roof trusses and was putting a beam along the peak of the roof. He hollered down to Jimmy, "Hey Jimmy, the blueprints call for a thirty-two-foot beam. But the roof is only thirty-one feet long. What do you want me to do?" Jimmy paused for a moment, then hollered back, "Chop it off."

I had learned why Jimmy was called *Chop-it-off.*

*****

One day, I was working with a crew putting finishing touches on a house. I needed to call Becky about plans for the evening. The house's phone wiring had been disconnected. When none of the other workers were around, I fiddled with the phone wiring using trial and error on it until I got a dial-tone. Then I called Becky. We talked, then I read her the number off of the faceplate on the phone I was calling from and told her she could call me back later if she needed to.

A couple hours later, the phone rang. Two carpenters stood by the ringing phone wondering if they should answer it. Finally, one of them picked it up. A moment later, more than slightly perplexed, he called me to the phone. After that phone call from Becky, I was teased by other workers for the rest of the afternoon about my love interests.

*****

Becky wanted to move away from Greensboro—to explore the world. She had friends in Portland, Oregon and thought it would be nice to live near them. She tried to talk me into leaving Greensboro with her.

We weren't in love—though we really enjoyed one another—and I was cautious. I didn't want to end up like Mike. After a while, I told Becky, "I have a close friend in Albuquerque. If I decide to move, I'll go there."

That was all Becky needed. She asked me if I would go west with her and decide, once we got to Albuquerque, whether we would continue on to Portland Oregon. She told me, using her best Mae West imitation, that I was her ticket out of town.

Toward the end of January, I agreed to drive to Albuquerque with Becky in her 1962 Rambler American. We would see what the future would bring when the future arrived—be that Albuquerque or Portland Oregon—and an ongoing relationship—or not. I gave notice at Dockery Lumber Company. My co-workers teased me about going west with a good-looking woman. It was good natured teasing and I enjoyed it.

*****

On my last day at work, Steve took me aside and said, "Show me your hands."

I put my hands in front of me, palms up. They were heavily calloused from months of intensely demanding work.

Steve looked at them and said, "If you show these hands to any construction company—anywhere—they'll offer you a job. Your hands show what you've done here; how hard you've worked".

I don't think anyone has ever said anything nicer to me about my work—anywhere—anytime.

*****

I had spent five months in Greensboro. It had been wonderful. But I had not succeeded in settling down. I said farewell to my sister, to Loretta and to others. I broke my apartment lease, gave my bicycle to Loretta—I am not really sure why I did that—and gave away or sold most of my other possessions.

6—On to Albuquerque

Being the daughter of a small city minister had its advantages when it came to shopping for a used car. When Becky told her dad she needed a car, he knew the proverbial little old lady who wanted to sell the car she had driven back-and-forth to the supermarket. While Ramblers weren't particularly cool-looking, this 1962 Nash Rambler Hardtop was like new. It had mileage of only thirty thousand miles, was in excellent mechanical condition, and the price was right.

Becky and I packed up the Rambler, put Ducky in the back seat, and headed west. It was mid-February of 1972. I was continuing my search for a home while Becky was relieved to be getting away from hers. We were both excited to be moving on to new adventures and enjoying the uncertainty that goes along with living day-to-day.

Traveling almost two thousand miles in a 1962 Nash Rambler hardtop meant not being in a hurry. The Rambler couldn't go much more than sixty miles-per-hour. As a result, there was no downside in riding on back roads. We appreciated the beauty of the picturesque countryside and the nuances of the small towns we passed through.

*****

As we crossed the southeast United States, we listened to AM radio stations. On a long car trip, AM radio puts you in touch with local communities. You hear their music, listen to their talk-radio banter and gain insight into their political values and religious beliefs. In between the lines, AM radio reveals a community's fears and dreams.

Garrison Keillor made a career out of small-town American radio culture. Keillor's show about Lake

Wobegon, *The Prairie Home Companion*, had always reminded me of the radio programs I listened to while growing up in rural Minnesota. Traveling with Becky, driving through those small southern towns, we experienced firsthand, the cultural richness that Keillor's program imitated.

We stopped in fascinating villages we would've never seen if we had been on the superhighway. Each had a story. The old theater, the neighborhood coffee shop, an abandoned gas station, general store or beautiful old school house—each rustic building hinted at a sub-plot that would never be revealed to us.

*****

Our limited funds meant we ate only at modestly priced restaurants that were full of local flavor. We generally camped in my tent or slept in the car—the Rambler's front seats folded back allowing us to stretch out.

On the first night of the journey, we camped at Stone Mountain State Park in Georgia. I set up my tent at a beautiful campsite under starry skies. The evening was so warm that I chose not to put the rainfly on the tent. We woke up at five the next morning. It had rained. Our sleeping bags had acted like sponges, absorbing water until they were saturated. We were cold, wet and laughing. We threw our soaked sleeping bags and tent into the backseat of the car— crowding Ducky a bit—and searched for a warm place in the village of Stone Mountain. We found a small café where we warmed ourselves while drinking coffee and eating eggs, country sausage and hominy grits with butter.

That minor fiasco could have been upsetting. But we just laughed. Instead of bringing us down, it ended up lifting us up. Our breakfast tasted so good that morning. Our waitress joined us in laughter after we told her of our rain-soaked night. After filling our bellies and warming our bodies, we found a laundromat, dried our sleeping bags, and were on our way. While we couldn't afford to eat many meals out, that breakfast had been sorely needed.

*****

The following day, we left Alabama heading into Southern Mississippi. Our route took us within thirty miles of Florida. I had been in forty-seven of the forty-eight continental states. I told Becky that if we made just a small detour, I could say I visited them all. Becky laughed at me and said she thought I was being pretty narcissistic. So, we bypassed Florida.

Later that day, we arrived in New Orleans where we faced two major housing challenges. The first was finding a place we could afford. The second was finding a place that allowed a dog. We ended up renting a small old trailer house in a rundown mobile home park fifteen minutes' drive from the French Quarter.

We relished those four days of Cajun music, Creole seafood, gin fizzes, Sazerac cocktails and mint juleps. We inhaled the rich ambience, the jazz, the historic architecture, liquor and atmosphere to such a degree that I can honestly say that while our stay was wonderful, my memories of it are quite hazy.

*****

After leaving New Orleans, we focused on getting to Albuquerque as quickly as possible. But the trip was still a pleasure. The sights and sounds between New Orleans and Albuquerque were captivating. We passed through a bayou country of lush swamps and waterways lined with moss covered trees—a huge contrast to the ugly oil refineries surrounding Houston that we passed later that day.

Beyond Houston and its endless suburban sprawl, we moved into the vast open ranges of Texas. The 600-mile drive from Houston to Amarillo took us past seemingly endless ranges of grass, wild flowers, cattle and oil derricks. The radio kept playing the song *A Horse with No Name*. The song's lyrics seemed to describe the country we were driving through.

> *There were plants and birds and rocks and things*
> *There was sand and hills and rings*
> *The first thing I met was a fly with a buzz*
> *And the sky with no clouds*
> *The heat was hot and the ground was dry*
> *But the air was full of sound*
> *I've been through the desert on a horse*
> *with no name...*

Becky laughed at the song's lyrics telling me that at some point in the future, I would describe our trip with those lyrics. She said I'd refer to her as the *horse with no name*.

*****

As we drove across the Texas rangeland, we passed a beautiful patch of wildflowers. I stopped the car; got out; and picked a small bouquet of red, yellow and blue flowers. Once back in the car, I gave the bouquet to Becky. She wept. Her tears totally confused me. Afterwards, she told me that no one had ever given her a bouquet of flowers. Hearing that humbled me.

I have fond memories of that drive. For both Becky and me, it was an expansion of life into uncertainty and adventure. We treated one another with kindness and affection. But, each of us had our own uncertainties.

*****

We drove straight through to Albuquerque catching only a few short naps at roadside rest stops along the way. We slept in the car rather than in my tent because we were afraid of rattlesnakes.

My classmate from Carleton, Russ was working as a janitor in a hospital and sharing a house with friends in Albuquerque. Before the trip, I wrote to him asking if we could stay at his house for a few days. He wrote back welcoming us.

Upon arrival in Albuquerque, we were tired and glad to get out of the car. Russ and his housemates made us feel welcome. Becky and I explored the city of Albuquerque and the mountains around it. We were stunned by the extraordinary breadth of desert colors—shades of burnt ochre and tan—and by the diverse textures found in those mountains.

We knew that we needed to make decisions—what was next for us? Becky wanted to continue on to Portland Oregon. I was afraid to make a long-term commitment. In any case until we had agreed on a plan for the future, we realized we had to figure out where we were going to live and how we would support ourselves.

*****

It was a challenge to find low-wage jobs in Albuquerque because the area had attracted so many young people. I found an advertisement for a taxi driver in *The Albuquerque Journal.* I called right away and got an interview. It didn't pay a lot and the hours were from 6PM to 6AM, but I needed a job. I agreed to start the following evening.

Later that day, I found an affordable room. The middle-aged woman who lived in and owned the house told me her primary concerns were that I would be a clean tenant but not be a bad influence on her young son. She quizzed me about my past and was satisfied with my responses. I rented the room.

*****

On my first night as a taxi driver, I rode with an experienced cabbie. He explained the protocols of picking up and charging customers, or *fares* as they were called. Navigating Albuquerque wasn't hard. The city was divided into four simple quadrants, each with an easy-to-learn set of sequential street names and numbers.

On my second shift, I was given the keys to a yellow cab. I was on my own.

Drivers were assigned fares by a taxi dispatcher over a shortwave radio system. Fares were supposed to be assigned based on a first taxi free gets the next fare. Thus, all taxi drivers on a given shift would earn similar amounts— theoretically. But as you might anticipate, friendships between dispatchers and cabbies meant that wasn't the case. Since I was dealing with a system I couldn't change, I didn't worry about it.

The cab company purchased and maintained vehicles and paid for all of their overhead. To cover its costs, the company retained sixty-percent of all fares. Taxi drivers kept the remaining forty-percent plus all tips.

Each fare was unique. Sometimes, a customer showed an interest in the driver. But generally, the driver was ignored. Some fares not only ignored their driver and didn't tip, they were just plain disrespectful. It was amazing to learn how a seemingly nice person could actually be such an arrogant jerk.

While my shift officially ended at six in the morning, there weren't a lot of fares after two. Rather than sit around earning nothing, drivers preferred to end their shift as early as possible. But not everyone could end their shift early. Our dispatcher would start calling in groups of taxis to close out their nights' work beginning at two.

A shortwave radio call by the dispatcher to a group of cabs started what amounted to a race between those cabbies. Whichever cab arrived at the dispatcher's office first was closed out first; its driver allowed to go home. Other cabbies were closed out in the order they arrived at the office. I have a clear memory of racing to the cab dispatcher's office in the middle of the night—at times at dangerous speeds—often ignoring stop signs and red lights—with the goal of being the first cab driver allowed to go home.

*****

As I look back at my time in Albuquerque, I realize I was not a great friend to Becky. When we got together in Greensboro, I needed a friend. She turned into one. She never asked for anything unreasonable. We always had a great time together—I don't remember a single argument. But in the end, my fears of ending up in a bad relationship were greater than my ability to be a friend. While I have no regrets about how my life has gone since, it is important to admit that I was selfish, fearful and shortsighted.

Becky wasn't devastated when I rented my own place. But my decision told her she needed to move forward with her life. She rented a small studio apartment for herself and Ducky. After I started working as a cab driver, she approached the taxi company and asked if they needed any more drivers. I am sure they found her to be an attractive candidate. And since taxi driving at night was especially dangerous, Becky was hired for the day-shift.

*****

I began to get to know some of the other drivers. I chatted with them before a shift, during meal breaks, while waiting at the bus station and at the end of each shift. Other cabbies shared tricks of the trade with me and asked about my background. And of course, everybody wanted to know about my relationship with Becky. Many of the night-shift drivers were quite interested in that new, cute, day-shift girl.

I began to learn the ropes of taxi-driving. My earnings were not great. But they were sufficient to cover my rent and other expenses. Becky and I would get together occasionally; sometimes for a meal break; other times on our days off. We would talk about our taxicab driving experiences. Most of Becky's prior jobs had been as a waitress in swanky restaurants. She was proud of being a cabby—and of her independence.

*****

One evening, I picked up a fare dressed in a wrinkled suit who was badly in need of a shave. He seemed distracted, mumbling confusing directions for wherever he wanted me to take him. As I drove, he continued to mumble. I pulled into a shopping mall parking lot to ask for a clarification of his destination. The man became agitated and reached inside his coat to pull something out. It looked to me like a handgun. I killed the motor, grabbed my key out of the ignition and ran.

As I ran, I saw, or imagined I saw, him kneeling on one knee. I was afraid he was aiming a gun at me. After I had gotten about fifty yards from the taxi, I stopped and looked back. I hoped he would leave the taxi; that I could get back into it. After a while, he did walk away from the cab. I circled the cab; ran back to it from the opposite direction; jumped in; and drove away.

After all of that, I took my meal break. I drove over to Becky's place; updating her on the evening's event; letting her know I no longer felt safe driving a cab; and telling her I was going to quit. Becky was sympathetic and supportive.

Then I asked, "Do you still want to drive west with me to Portland?"

Becky said, "No." Then she paused for a moment before completing her thought. "There was a time—not long ago—when I wanted to drive to Portland with you. You said *no*. Now, I am finally feeling good about the independence I've created for myself. It was what I wanted—what I needed. You've been a good friend. Thank you for that. But I am not ready to leave Albuquerque."

A half an hour later, I drove my cab into the taxi garage where I told the dispatcher what had happened and informed him that I was quitting.

*****

My taxi cab driving experience in Albuquerque gave me good reasons to respect the people who perform the difficult and dangerous low-wage job of driving a cab. They work under intense and often unsafe conditions. And they are often treated with disrespect by their customers.

*****

When I was a student in college, I had a reputation for going on trips at the last minute without giving anyone any advanced notice. Sometimes those trips just were just visits to my grandparents fifty miles away. Other times, they were a lot longer. Once, I left campus the day before final exams. In that instance, I was fortunate. My professors gave me a second chance to take final exams after I returned. My friends used to call these unanticipated, unplanned and poorly communicated trips *pulling a Roger*. While I wasn't the only one who had ever pulled a Roger, I was certainly the creator and the master of the art form.

So, when I told Russ I was moving on, he wished me the best. But he was not surprised. I was simply pulling a Roger. It wasn't that he didn't care about our friendship. He understood that oftentimes my response to situations that were difficult to manage was to leave, maybe more correctly, to run away. In any case, Russ accepted that I was leaving. Before I left, we talked about maybe getting a place together in some other city at some point in the future. Our conversation was vague. Nothing was decided.

*****

My mother lived in Denver Colorado, just a few hundred miles north of Albuquerque. It seemed like a good time for me to visit her and my brother John. From there, I decided I might travel east and live near my dad in New York.

But it would be an exaggeration to say my plan was firm.

*****

Becky and I had not fallen in love with one another. But she had been a wonderful friend. After she drove me to the bus station a couple of days later, our goodbye was a little sad. But each of us was ready to move on.

7—Time with Mom

As I rode on the Greyhound Bus heading to Denver, I thought about the upcoming visit with my mother. I reflected on the changes that had taken place in me and in my family over the past few years. Since my parents' separation, my dad had moved forward in his life and my mother had tried to rebuild hers.

When my parents separated on New Year's Day of 1965, my sister Diane was eighteen, I was fifteen and my brother Johnny was three. My father was president of the State College in Moorhead, Minnesota. He was the most respected person in our community. As the president's wife, my mother had had an important role and had been treated with respect by all.

No choice was required, but after my parents separated, each friend of the family did make a choice whether they were going to continue a friendship with my father, the college president, for whom many of them worked—or with my mom, who no longer had standing in the community. Almost all of them made the obvious safe choice. They decided to be a friend to my father and to write off my mother.

The situation was painful for me. One surreal personal memory stands out. In early 1965, I went shopping for groceries with my mother. I saw a family friend—someone who had previously had a warm relationship with both of my parents. When this man saw me, he quickly turned away; probably hoping I hadn't seen him. It wasn't rare to have someone look away from my mother and me during that period. What was unique was that the next day,

I was in the same supermarket, and this time with my father. I saw the same man. He walked up to me and said, "Roger. How wonderful to see you."

Over the years, I have often pondered that chance meeting. Because my dad was president of the college, it was not surprising that this man had chosen to befriend my father. But I have always been amazed at the sheer hypocrisy of his behavior—his lack of shame as he looked away from me one day, then welcomed me with open arms the next.

*****

In the spring of 1967, as my graduation from high school approached, I was ready to go away to college. But I was also more than ready to say goodbye to Moorhead. I realized my mother should leave the community as well and tried to talk her into moving to Minneapolis where her parents, sister and an assortment of other friends and relatives lived. She refused. Moving back to the city in which she had grown up after her life had fallen apart was just too shameful. I told my mom that if she decided to stay in Moorhead, I would not live with her during that summer after graduation or visit here there during college breaks. I was done with Fargo-Moorhead.

Less than three months before I graduated from high school, my mother, brother and I were driving back from a visit to my grandparents in Minneapolis. My mother turned to me and said, "How about moving to San Francisco?"

We had never even considered the possibility of moving to California, but I knew that it had always had romantic allure for her. I looked at her and said, "We've got a deal".

When we arrived at our home in Moorhead, my mom called my sister Diane, a student at the University of Iowa.

When Diane heard our plan, she said, "If you can delay the move to San Francisco until I graduate in June, I'll go with you."

So, in late June of 1967, my sister, brother, mom and I traveled cross-country to San Francisco in my mom's 1962 Oldsmobile Dynamic 88. Our rooftop carrier was packed with our belongings. Our hearts were full of great expectations—and a lot of sadness.

San Francisco was an exciting place to live during that summer of 1967. It was the *Summer of Love*. In addition to working as a busboy at a restaurant on Market Street, I explored the city and took in the excitement of Haight-Ashbury.

But the summer ended. I was off to college and my sister moved to New York City. But my mother and brother remained in San Francisco for three and a half years. During most of that time, they were alone and my mom showed a strength and resiliency that was fairly astounding. She found a job and created a life for my brother and herself. When her employer moved his office from San Francisco to Denver, my mom kept her job with the company and moved there as well. In San Francisco, my mother had rented an apartment. In Denver, she purchased a home.

My brother Johnny is twelve years younger than I. We have always been very close. My short visit to Denver was going to be a chance to catch up and have fun with him. As the bus neared Denver, spending time with Johnny was foremost in my mind.

*****

I had not seen my mother since graduating from college. As soon as I arrived, it was clear she hoped I would stay in Denver and become part of her life. She offered to turn her garage into an apartment for me and help me purchase a used car. She would fix me up with a nice Jewish girl and hoped I would find a job that would make her proud of me—a work position offering financial stability.

My mother's dreams and mine did not align. I was searching for meaning. She wanted to assist me in finding security—while living close to her. I understood and appreciated why my mom wanted me to stay in Denver. But my need to move forward in my life was stronger than any guilt my mother could lay on to keep me there.

I stayed in Denver for two weeks. During the visit, I was treated royally. Saying goodbye to my mother and brother was painful. In retrospect, they were both incredibly respectful of my decision to continue my search. However, decades later, it's still painful to consider how they must've felt as I departed.

8—Upstate New York

I had not lived near my dad since leaving Moorhead five years before. In fact, I hadn't spent much time with him in seven years. When I'd visited him the prior fall, my father told me if I moved to New Paltz, I would find job opportunities. I decided to explore them.

*****

The road from Colorado to New York can be cold during the early spring. For that reason, I decided to take a Greyhound Bus to New York. The trip was uneventful. However, one conversation stands out.

As the bus traversed the snowy countryside of Pennsylvania, I sat next to an elderly woman. She spoke to me about spending her life farming in rural Ohio. I asked if she felt farming was a life worth pursuing. I remember her heartfelt response.

"You realize you are asking a question of someone with a bias. I lived off the land all my life. Now you ask me if farming is something I'd recommend to someone else? My response is simple. The land is next to God."

This woman had found peace in growing things. She lived her life in accord with what had meaning for her. She had found her *it*.

To be successful in my voyage of self-discovery, I had to determine what that *it* was for me. My journey was far from complete.

*****

My father and Sally welcomed me to New York by taking me out to a German restaurant for a wonderful Wiener schnitzel dinner. The warmth of the welcome did not remove my hard feelings towards Sally—I had been taught to blame her for my parents' divorce. But as time passed, I learned to not blame Sally for their problems. And, she turned out to be a very interesting person—one who always treated me in a warm and gracious manner.

The morning after my arrival, my dad sat down with me to discuss my job search. Friends and family often offer help in finding a job. More often than not, the help is encouragement without practical value. That was not the case in this instance. My father offered concrete suggestions that demonstrated his understanding of my voyage of self-discovery. He did not ask me to search for a job that would lead to a successful career. He was proud that my job search was not about ambition—that I had chosen to pursue understanding rather than riches.

My dad knew the owner of a small resort that was a short drive from his home. The resort was about to start hiring for its summer season. He suggested I apply for a job at the resort. It seemed like an opportunity worth exploring.

Built on the shores of a mountain lake, the Resort at Lake Minnewaska was twenty minutes from New Paltz in the Shawangunk Mountains. Its property included thousands of acres of wilderness, horse stables, trails and winter skiing facilities. The lake offered swimming and the use of canoes and rowboats. When the resort was established in the 1870s, its New York City clientele traveled from the Big Apple to the resort in a single day. They began the trip on rail and finished it on horse-drawn carriages. In 1870, Minnewaska's forests and streams were full of wild game. The world had changed a lot in the intervening century but the serenity of the resort was retained.

A week after arriving in New Paltz, I borrowed my dad's car and drove to Minnewaska. I was interviewed by the resort owner's son, a man in his thirties who served as general manager. He explained that each spring, in anticipation of its busy season, Minnewaska hired forty or fifty young people to fill summer jobs. He offered me a job as a chauffeur. It didn't pay a lot—about forty dollars per week—but I'd receive room and board and have access to the resort's lake, trails and other facilities. Since I'd have few other expenses while living there, most of what I earned would be saved. What a great way to recharge my batteries! I accepted the position. A couple of days later, I moved into the resort's employee housing.

*****

Minnewaska had two 19th century hotel buildings. Every room in each hotel had wonderful views of either the mountain lake or of the surrounding countryside. The hotels were stately and included original furniture—solid, simple, wooden and elegant. The Cliff House was the older hotel. Its architecture and furniture designs were Victorian. The other hotel, Wildmere, was built just before the turn of the century. It's architecture and furniture were classic Arts and Crafts.

When I was hired, all hotel guests were housed at Wildmere. The Cliff House had not been updated to meet fire code. So, even though it was picturesque, fully furnished and incredibly cool, it stood empty.

*****

Describing my time at Minnewaska without commenting on the resort's management team would ignore the chaos that made working there such a frolicsome adventure. For being employed at the resort was like being in the cast of an Oscar Wilde play.

Ken Sr., the bustling owner and manager of Minnewaska purchased the resort in 1955. He was chubby, short and ran around as if her were pantomiming *so much to do; so little time*. Ken Sr. was energetic and a poor communicator. He was a slightly overweight, middle-aged version of Charlie Chaplin.

His son, Ken Jr., looked like a younger version of his father. However, Ken Jr. had gone to business school, was able to communicate and viewed the resort business with a much broader perspective than his father. But it was impossible for Ken Jr. to manage the resort to his dad's plan because I'm fairly certain his dad had no plan.

Ken Jr. was married to a former beauty queen, a lovely woman who was gracious to everyone—including me. It must have been a lonely life for her in that isolated location which was dominated by her father in-law.

Ken Sr.'s daughter, Paula, was about thirty and loved horses. She spent most of her time taking care of those horses and was not highly involved in running the resort.

The resort employed two administrative employees, a personnel manager and a bookkeeper.

After Ken Jr. hire me, I met with the personnel manager. He was open about his perspectives on Minnewaska. In a nutshell, he'd worked at the resort for almost a year and fallen in love with a waitress to whom he was about to be married. His primary achievement at Minnewaska had been falling in love.

Margaret, the bookkeeper, was about seventy years old. She had the personality and appearance of a tree stump. Margaret never had a friendly word to say to anyone, especially me. She completed the cartoonesque management staffing of Lake Minnewaska.

*****

The resort was largely a seasonal operation. It had few guests and few employees between the months of November and April. Most of the maintenance, front desk, housekeeping and restaurant workers were hired in May and June. Some employees worked in Florida's resorts in the winter. But most of the employees were college students from throughout the country. For them, Minnewaska was sort of an advanced summer camp.

The dishwashers were a separate group. They were New York City indigents who had drinking problems. I was told that Ken Sr. hired these men off the street in New York City. They were asked to stay on resort property during their employment out of fear that if they ever went to town, they would get drunk and be arrested.

When I was hired, the resort had fifty employees and fifteen guests—an unusual ratio. In spite of the lack of guests, the personnel manager was continuing to offer jobs to college students across the country. That seemed odd to me. But of course, I had no business education.

*****

As a chauffeur, my job was to transport guests to the resort from local train depots, bus stations and New York City airports. Then, I returned them when their stay was complete. I also drove guests to local tourist destinations and provided whatever other transportation support the resort or its guests needed (including occasionally picking up food supplies at a nearby grocery). The resort had two Chrysler New Yorker extended length limousines that were used for these purposes.

A couple of days after I was hired, Minnewaska hosted a weekend conference for psychologists from across the country. The day before the conference, I raced back and forth to New York City airports, picking up five or six psychologists at a time. Ken Sr. also ferried guests to and from the airports in his plush, late model Lincoln Continental. On my second trip into the city, I decided to make my ride more interesting by picking up a hitchhiking college student. He was pretty impressed when a limousine pulled over to the side of the road and offered him a ride. The student and I had a nice conversation and everything was going quite nicely until I noticed a Lincoln Continental had pulled up next to me. Its driver, Ken Sr., signaled extreme displeasure.

Ken Sr. pulled into a toll booth ahead of me. When I arrived at the toll booth, the toll taker said, "The driver of the car ahead of you asked me to pass on a message. *Lose the hitchhiker.* Then you're supposed to follow him to the airport. The guy said he has a few shortcuts."

My hitchhiker was left standing at the toll booth. I had to drive furiously to keep up with Ken Sr. who drove to Kennedy Airport like a bat out of hell; swerving between lanes; either trying to beat all records for getting to the airport or trying to lose me—probably both. By then, I was appropriately intimidated for having been caught with a hitchhiker. I followed the Lincoln Continental closely—like glue on a stamp.

When we got to the airport, Ken Sr. got out of his car, briskly walked up to my car and said to me, "First of all, if you are going to drive for me, never pick up another hitchhiker! Secondly," he paused while I wondered what was coming, "you're a pretty good driver!"

*****

Two weeks after I started at Minnewaska, a second chauffeur was hired. There wasn't enough work for one chauffeur, but the resort had always hired two. So why stop now? Robert, the new chauffeur, was a couple of years younger than me. He had a good sense of humor and I enjoyed working with him.

Robert and I often drove to New Paltz. On the way, there was a five- or six-mile stretch of rural highway that was straight and level. I often drove that stretch at ninety-five miles per hour, a healthy thirty-five miles per hour above the speed limit. During his second week at Minnewaska, Robert got two speeding tickets for driving eighty miles per hour on that stretch.

A day or two later, Ken Sr. quietly pulled me aside and told me about Robert's misfortune. "State Patrol officers have spotted one of our Chryslers racing at even higher speeds on the drive between the Resort and New Paltz. Each time the patrol officers saw the speeding limousine, it was from a distance and going so fast that the officers were not able to catch it. We both know that you and Robert drive identical cars. I suspect it was you going at those high speeds. They were just able to catch Robert. You need to be more careful."

I took Ken Sr.'s advice seriously and never got a traffic ticket.

*****

Sometimes, I took guests on a tour of the area. One of the most interesting local sights was the historic architecture of Huguenot Street in New Paltz. Several of its buildings were constructed by French Huguenot immigrants in the early 1720's using rugged stone materials unlike those in any other architecture I'd seen.

I was driving three resort guests to see the buildings. One of the guests, a confident but sour woman, began to talk to me like I was an idiot. Her arrogance was not only offensive to me, the other guests were uncomfortably quiet.

I slowly pulled the car over to the side of the road; put it in park; then turned around and faced the woman. "I am sorry ma'am," I said politely. "There is no room in this car for condescension." I calmly turned back to the steering wheel and continued the tour. The woman said nothing more for the rest of the drive.

*****

I had several fascinating interludes with guests. Once I ferried members of a wedding party between events. In the morning, I picked up the bride and her bridesmaids and drove them to a small local church for the wedding ceremony. While I drove, I listened to their prattle, astonished at its superficiality. The major items of discussion were the size of her ring and her fiancé's wealth.

Later that day, I drove the newly married couple to their reception. It was obvious that the groom was terribly bored with his new bride. While she chattered, he gazed out his window, appearing painfully uninterested.

*****

Living where you work simplifies making friends— they are your co-workers. My time at the resort became a satisfying social experience. In particular, there were two young women I enjoyed getting to know. They were straight forward, open and without guile. I enjoyed laughing, talking about life and gossiping about guests with them.

One of these women had borrowed a 1959 Triumph sports car. She let me drive it into New Paltz. It's funny how a decades old memory of something as insignificant as driving around in a cool car for half an hour can bring back a wave of good feelings. I enjoyed shifting gears as I maneuvered the car along a mountain road though I did grind them a few times. The car rode so close to the ground that, as I drove it through a bumpy New Paltz parking lot, I scraped the car's bottom against the asphalt.

*****

Ken Jr. allowed me to use the resort's 1967 Cadillac Coupe Deville for personal trips. Sometimes I drove it on days off to visit my dad. But I wanted to purchase my own car. A resort employee offered to sell me his 1962 Volvo sedan. Early 1960s Volvos were legendary for their streamlined design and quality engines. They were also regarded as hip. The employee told me it was mine for five hundred dollars. That seemed like an incredible value. But I didn't have the money. I asked my father if he would lend me five hundred dollars to buy the car. It didn't seem like a lot to borrow and I felt having a car would be nice.

My father said, "I don't think so Roger. Buying a car is something you should be able to do with money you've already saved—or you should be in a position where you can afford regular car payments—in addition, of course, to gas and insurance. I just don't think you're there. It wouldn't be fair for me to put you in a financial bind by lending you that five hundred dollars."

My dad had always been generous. I'd never asked for a loan before. I was disappointed. However, as I look back at his decision, I realize he was wise—and courageous. He wanted my trust, but wasn't willing to do something he felt didn't make sense in order to earn it. He was right. I was not in a position to pay the operating costs of a car. Purchasing a car at that time would have forced me to change the way I was living in order to earn enough to pay my expenses. Owning a car was not the right thing for me at that time.

***** *****

As I look back at my career as a Minnewaska chauffeur, I admit to my immaturity. But Ken Sr. and Ken Jr. were quite pleased with the compliments they were receiving from guests about the service I was delivering. They were so pleased that when the personnel manager resigned (to marry his sweetheart), they offered me the position of personnel manager. They would increase my pay to seventy dollars a week plus room and board and let me use the Cadillac Coupe Deville whenever I wanted.

I was caught off guard. I had been comfortable at the bottom of the organizational structure and had definitely not sought a promotion. However, I didn't spend a lot of time analyzing whether I should accept the position or not. Over the prior year, I had allowed the winds of change to blow me where they might. This was just another fresh breeze. I accepted the position. After being at the resort for less than six weeks, I was its personnel manager with my own office.

***** *****

Now that I was management, Ken Jr. encouraged me to move out of regular staff housing. I took a corner room on the fourth floor of the Cliff House. Through its windows, I could gaze across hundreds of acres of wooded countryside with a range of mountains in the distance. My room was furnished with an old iron bed, an antique wooden dresser, a dressing table, and a century-old wood rocker with a hand-woven wicker seat. The ambience of the room was completed by faded flower-patterned wallpaper as old as the hotel.

I was the only person staying in that large century-old hotel. When I awoke in the middle of the night, I never identified noises I could prove were from ghosts wandering its hallways. But I would wake up in the middle of the night and think about it.

*****

I had had no management training or experience. But I was able to use common sense. It was the end of June. There were seventy employees at Minnewaska—and the same number of guests. The resort had made job commitments to an additional ten college students who hadn't yet arrived. While I had no register of employees. Once I created such a list, I took it to Ken Jr. and told him we had too many employees. He authorized me to make changes.

I telephoned the ten students who had been offered employment, but had not yet arrived. I told them we had to recant on our offer of employment. Two or three of them took this bad news without protest. The others were either devastated or furious. I listened to what each of them had to say. But there wasn't workload to justify employing them. I also spoke with several local employees and told them we couldn't continue to employ them.

*****

Once I had addressed staffing levels, there wasn't much for me to do. I had no supervisory role and I had time to kill. A special benefit of my job was freshly baked pastries. Our pastry chef was a fine Viennese gentleman who produced wonderful pastries. I could walk down to his pastry kitchen and get fresh and delicate buttery pastries anytime I wanted. I often distracted myself on slow days by visiting him. I ate more pastry than I should have and gained ten pounds in one month. But I loved every bite.

*****

At one point, Ken Sr.'s daughter Paula asked if I would interview her friend for a job in housekeeping. When an owner's family member asks you to interview somebody, you interview them. The woman came to the job interview looking like a fashion model—tall, thin, and stylishly dressed in black knee-high riding boots, tight pants and an expensive loosely fitting white silk blouse. This woman probably had never made a bed. But she said she wanted to become a maid. I chatted with her for a while, then politely told her we just didn't have any openings.

In retrospect, I believe Paula was trying to introduce me to her friend. My simplistic response speaks to my less than advanced social skills.

*****

Being in a management position became a barrier between me and other employees. Some were put off by the fact that I was *management*. Others felt that because I was their friend, I should promote them into a better paying position. After all, it wouldn't cost me anything.

The job ended up isolating me.

*****

Kens Sr. and Jr. continued to listen to my recommendations. While, I had no business training, many of my common-sense suggestions were implemented and helped improve operations at the resort.

Ken Sr. rarely complimented the staff, but was quick to criticize them when he felt like it. He believed that if you pay too many compliments to a worker, it goes to their head.

As a result, most resort employees felt unappreciated and did not like him.

I took a different tack. I would approach a worker who was doing a good job and say that Ken Sr. had told me he was impressed with the good work that that the employee was doing. But, I added, "he's just too shy to say it." Ken Sr. would have been livid if he knew what I had been saying. But he thanked me for the increase in employee morale.

*****

One day when both Ken Sr. and Ken Jr. were off-site, I was called to the kitchen. A drunken dishwasher was threatening anyone who came near him. I walked up to him and told him he had to leave the kitchen—he couldn't threaten other workers. Hearing that, he picked up a large carving knife and came after me, chasing me for several minutes before some other employees distracted him. I wanted him taken from the resort before he hurt someone, particularly me. I went back to my office and called Paula asking her to immediately authorize his final payroll check. She said it was a busy time and asked if it could wait. I said, "No. I need the check now."

I picked up the signed payroll check and took it to another employee who drove the drunken dishwasher to New Paltz. Afterwards, as I walked into the dining room, I heard Margaret the bookkeeper complaining about what a pain in the ass I was. She had evidently heard my phone conversation with Paula.

In a self-righteous tone, Margaret said, "Everything is always a rush with him!"

I walked into the dining room and said loudly and clearly, "Margaret, you are a fish!"

Margaret did not respond.

*****

The wall between me and other employees continued to grow and I enjoyed my job less and less. Being management was not as much fun as being a worker and I was not accomplishing anything meaningful.

I visited my father and shared with him that I was miserable. He said to me, "Growing up as I did in Nazi Germany, I looked forward to turning twenty-one years of age hoping that when I became an adult, my problems would go away. However, when I turned twenty-one, after leaving Nazi Germany and coming to this country, instead of going away, the number and size of my problems appeared to grow. It wasn't until a few years ago that I came to realize that life is really made of small things. If you are able to put together enough small things that have meaning, your life becomes full."

That advice has always struck me as deeply insightful. I will never forget it.

*****

After a month as Minnewaska's personnel manager, Ken Jr. approached me to talk about my future with the resort. I had signed on as a summer employee. Ken Jr. said that he and his father wanted me to stay on with Minnewaska an ongoing basis. They liked the work I was doing. He told me they were ready to increase my salary to one hundred dollars per week and add health benefits. But they wanted me to sign a contract committing to stay with the resort for at least a year. I told Ken Jr. I would think about it.

That offer was the first time anyone had asked me for what I considered to be a long (one whole year) commitment. I considered my options for a few days. While

I was flattered with the offer, I realized I had not even begun to achieve my goal of finding personal truth. I had not figured out what my *it* was.

Minnewaska was always in a state of chaos. I decided my leaving would not make things worse. A few days after receiving the offer, I told Ken Jr. I would be resigning. Ken Jr. was gracious in accepting my decision. I agreed to stay until a replacement was hired.

*****

I had remained in touch with Russ who was still in Albuquerque. He had written to me that he was considering leaving Albuquerque to study medicine—maybe at the University of Michigan. I wrote back telling him I was leaving Minnewaska. I asked if he wanted to share an apartment in Michigan while he got his degree. He wrote back saying he liked the idea.

I had a plan.

Three weeks later, Minnewaska hired a replacement. I was once again happily unemployed and looking forward to my next adventure. I bid farewell to my father, put on my backpack, stuck out my thumb, and headed west to meet Russ.

9—Heading to Michigan

Russ and I planned to meet in Minneapolis. We intended to hitchhike north and take a camping trip in the Boundary Waters Canoe Area. After that, we would travel to Ann Arbor, Michigan where we'd get an apartment, find jobs and Russ could begin enrollment at the University of Michigan.

*****

Hitchhiking to Minneapolis took me across New Jersey, Pennsylvania, Ohio and into Chicago where a college friend was in a post-graduate program at the University of Illinois. I was taking my friend up on his offer of a night's lodging if I ever passed through his city. Roger (his name also) had graduated from Carleton in my class with a clear plan of what he wanted to achieve and how he would achieve it. Step one was getting his masters. Step two was getting a PhD. And because becoming a naturalist required in-the-field experience, step three would be establishing a national reputation working with wild animals. While he achieved these goals, he would also marry his true love, Constance.

I arrived at Roger's apartment late in the evening. He fixed us an excellent dinner and I had a good night's rest. Then, early the next morning, Roger walked me to a good intersection where I would begin my day's hitchhiking. On our way, we walked down a quiet urban street and I let out a holler of joy—I was feeling good!

Roger, who I believed didn't think too much of me, said, "That's the thing I admire about you—it's something I just can't do." I was totally confused. Was he being sarcastic? I asked him what he meant.

He explained. "The price of pursuing my career goals has been that I could not allow myself the freedom to act spontaneously. I don't even know if I'm capable of hollering out at life while walking down a city street in the early morning. I don't think I could hitchhike across the country without a schedule or if I could decide to start a life in a new town without a single friend or job prospect. I gave up that kind of freedom when I committed to my career plan."

Sometimes, one is humbled by another person's humility and honesty. While I pretend I'm not competitive, that just isn't true. To have Roger pay me that unqualified compliment, when he could quite easily have looked down upon me as a flake going nowhere—well, that humbled me. It caused me to respect him for a level of candor, integrity and humility of which I probably wasn't capable.

*****

I arrived in Minneapolis ahead of Russ. I was looking forward to spending time with my grandparents. My early arrival gave me the time to go to the Shriners Hall with my grandfather to play pool and have lunch and to sit down with my grandmother at her dining room table, drink coffee and listen to her tell stories about her life.

*****

My grandfather was smuggled out of what is now Romania when he was five years old. He made his way with a sister and brother-in-law to Minneapolis to join his father who was already working for the Great Northern Railway. His father, my great-grandfather, had planned that his entire family would join them in Minneapolis. His wife, my great-grandmother and their two older sons intended to come to this country. But because one son had a deformed leg, he could not get a visa to enter this country. So, my

114

great-grandmother and her other son decided to stay with him in their shtetl in Romania.

In the early 1940s, Nazis took Jewish villagers from that shtetl to a nearby wooded area where they were forced to dig a ditch. Once the ditch was dug, the Nazis shot the Jews and then pushed their bodies into the ditch which they had just dug. Those murdered Shtetl Jews included my great-grandmother and her two sons

*****

My grandmother was born and raised in a northern Wisconsin two-room log cabin which her family shared with their milk cows. Her father was a farmer in the spring, summer and fall. But during the winter, he was a logger. My grandmother's childhood experience was similar to the childhood of Laura Ingalls Wilder as described in her book *Little House in the Woods*.

*****

My grandmother met my grandfather in 1919 when she and her sister Theresa—both fresh off the farm—were walking down Hennepin Avenue in Minneapolis. The two girls spotted a couple of stylish young men. My grandmother told Theresa, "I'll take the one with the bell bottoms." Within months, my grandparents were living together. They never fell out of love. For me, their love has always been the gold standard of marriages.

*****

Shortly after Russ arrived in Minneapolis, we got together and quickly refined our camping plan. We would hitchhike to Ely, Minnesota; rent a canoe; then buy food and supplies to compliment the basic camping equipment we already owned. Our costs for the trip would be modest.

The Boundary Waters Canoe Area is located along the northern border of Minnesota. The park includes over one million acres of forests, lakes, rivers and is full of wildlife. I lived in Hibbing, near the Boundary Waters Canoe Area, until I was eight. During summers, my family stayed in a cabin my parents constructed themselves on the shores of a wilderness lake. For me, camping in the wild beauty of the Boundary Waters Canoe Area would be like going back to a special time in my childhood. Russ, who had been raised in Colorado and loved the outdoors, was as enthusiastic as I was about our trip to the north country.

*****

Sometimes, when you begin a trip without a great deal of planning, it turns into a mild nightmare. (See my adventure on the Appalachian Trail). That was not the case on this voyage in the Border Water Canoe Area. Once we arrived in Ely, the outfitters mapped out an interesting and challenging ten-day excursion. Their van transported us, along with a canoe, equipment and food supplies to within a quarter mile of a river onto which we launched our canoe. Within a couple hours of being left off by the outfitters, we were quietly and peacefully paddling our way down this small river which quickly opened into a large lake.

Late August nights are cold in northern Minnesota. But the advantage of that was we ran into few other campers and even fewer mosquitoes. We spent ten days paddling, portaging, camping and enjoying untouched lakes and forests. We saw Indian paintings on rock walls, wildlife and unending wilderness beauty. One night, we were deluged by a monumental thunderstorm. The rain came down in torrents and the lightning didn't stop until the sun rose. But my little tent kept us dry. We canoed twenty-six miles, portaged another two miles and improved our canoeing and camping skills to the degree where we were certain we could have successfully raced against Lewis and Clark.

Refreshed from the canoe trip and ready for anything that would come our way, we headed for Ann Arbor. Our blue highway/deep forested route would take us through Duluth, across northern Wisconsin and into the Upper Peninsula of Michigan. There, we would turn south at the Straits of Mackinac. The last leg of our road to Ann Arbor would be fast and direct on an interstate highway.

Sounds straightforward, doesn't it?

*****

The hitchhiking trip didn't go as smoothly as the canoe trip. Even though the countryside was as beautiful as we had hoped, hitchhiking will rarely be as peaceful as canoeing down wilderness rivers or across serene lakes. A couple hours after leaving Ely, we stopped for a lunch of peanut butter and jelly sandwiches. After a couple of bites of my sandwich, I got the hiccups.

My father used to have severe bouts of hiccups that would last for hours. Sometimes he would have serial hiccups—three or four consecutive-chain hiccups without a moment's break. I am ashamed to say that while he endured that pain, my sister and I laughed and my mom giggled. In between hiccups, my father would swear in German.

I had gotten hiccups from time to time, but never really appreciated how horrible they could be until the summer of 1970 when, as a counselor at a YMCA camp in northern Minnesota, I hiccupped for three days—nonstop. When the hiccups started, they were a distraction. After a few hours, they began to tire me out. By the end of the first day of hiccups, I was emotionally and physically exhausted. During the third day, it all seemed like a bad dream.

On that third day in 1970, the YMCA camp called in a doctor who gave me a shot of Thorazine, a powerful drug which just plain knocks you out. Thorazine is so powerful that it is given to people during bad hallucinogenic drug experiences as an anti-psychotic. After the doctor gave me a shot of Thorazine at the YMCA camp, I walked back to my cabin, got into bed and slept for eighteen hours. When I woke up, I felt great—and my hiccups were gone.

However, as I was hitch-hiking across Wisconsin and Michigan, I did not have access to the YMCA camp doctor. I just couldn't stop those hiccups. So, Russ and I continued hitchhiking—with my hiccups. When we arrived in Ann Arbor, our plan was to find an apartment and jobs. But I needed to get rid of those hiccups. After looking at apartments-for-rent ads in newspapers and on campus bulletin boards, we had to admit that housing in Ann Arbor was just plain expensive. We decided to rent a motel room for a couple of days while we figured out how to proceed. We found an affordable motel, grabbed an inexpensive dinner and tried to get a good night rest.

I had hoped that a good night's sleep would stop the hiccups. But it didn't. I continued to hiccup and did not sleep at all. The next morning—my third day of hiccups—I decided to go to an emergency room. The emergency room doctor's solution was similar to what I received at the YMCA camp. He gave me four Thorazine pills. His direction was to take one pill and wait to see if it stopped the hiccups. After four hours, if I still had hiccups, I could take another pill. After another four hours, if they hadn't gone away, I was to take the final two pills.

We got back to the motel. I took a pill, laid down to rest, and continued to hiccup. After an hour I took the second pill. Once more, I waited an hour and there was no change. Then, I took the final two pills. I had taken all four pills within a three-hour period. I finally fell asleep but the hiccups didn't stop. Russ told me that every time I hiccupped, my arms would flail, my body would heave—but the hiccups did not abate. Finally, the hiccups stopped and I went into a deep sleep.

Russ began to worry about whether the dosage of Thorazine I'd taken was dangerous. He called up a poison center hotline and told them how much Thorazine I had taken over a three-hour period. Russ asked for their recommendation.

The poison center hotline staff person told him, "Your friend is nuts, but he is going to be okay."

That observation could be used to describe much of my life.

*****

Having dispensed with hiccups, I slept well and started out the day ready to find a job and an apartment. Neither Russ nor I had anticipated the competitive rush for jobs and housing in a large college town. We found that many fall-term apartment leases had been signed in June and most job vacancies had been filled.

As we spoke with people about housing and jobs, it became clear that many students at the University of Michigan were from affluent backgrounds. In fact, I had never been around such an arrogant group of young, upper-middle-class and confident people. Not only was the rent for the few available apartments high and the availability of jobs low, but every student we spoke with treated us as if we were social outcasts. They were scholars at a great university and we were not. One Ann Arbor unpleasant moment would follow another. Each interchange with one of these young overconfident creeps was seemingly worse than the last.

Adding insult to injury, landlords seemed to look at us with distrust. We were not students and did not have jobs. The fact that we were not ready to make a three-month deposit at rent levels double or triple what we had anticipated made us look like we were high risk tenants.

*****

We needed jobs, an affordable place to live and Russ needed to take a couple of pre-med courses before starting medical school. Then, an inspired solution hit us. Why not go into the inner-city of Detroit? We could live in a place that wasn't dominated by rich, arrogant white kids, find jobs and rent an affordable apartment. And Russ could complete his pre-med classwork at Detroit's Wayne State University.

We packed our bags, walked to the bus station, and boarded a bus to Detroit. This was going to be a new adventure!

*****

Neither Russ nor I had ever been to Detroit. We didn't know exactly what to expect. We were just certain that the elitism that was so prevalent in Ann Arbor would not be an issue in The Motor City.

Our first priority in Detroit was for Russ to register at Wayne State University for winter quarter, 1973. A couple of hours after our Greyhound Bus arrived in Detroit, we were in Wayne State University's admissions office. Russ filled out an admissions application, attached a copy of his transcript and turned the paperwork over to a receptionist.

After a short wait, Russ was introduced to an admissions officer who listened to Russ' plan, reviewed his transcript, and explained that Russ' plan had been a good one—with one single glaring issue. Winter term admissions had closed the previous week.

Then the admissions officer added, "On the other hand, I would be a fool to turn away an applicant who just graduated magna cum laude from Carleton College."

The admissions officer backdated Russ' application by a week and checked a box next to the phrase *Admitted for Winter Quarter*.

*****

Our first challenge in Detroit had been successfully navigated. Within an hour, we found an inexpensive motel room near Wayne State University and focused upon finding an affordable place to live.

We asked a desk clerk at our motel about apartments in nearby neighborhoods. He told us that before a lot of folks moved to the suburbs, the area around the General Motors Building had housed thousands of General Motors staff. Its attractive brick and concrete buildings, built in the nineteen-twenties and thirties, had a lot of affordable, good-quality apartments. But the desk clerk (who was not a person of color) added that the area was now dangerous. He encouraged us to move out to Dearborn or one of the other "safe" suburbs.

Russ and I figured that *safe* was a code word for white. We'd come from Ann Arbor to escape that sort of insulation. We walked the short distance to the General Motors Building and started searching for an apartment. There were quite a few vacancy signs in apartment building windows. After a day of looking, we found a really nice third floor apartment for one hundred dollars a month. It surpassed our every expectation in every regard. But the nicest feature was a sunroom surrounded by exterior windows.

Just before we agreed to take the apartment, Russ said, "I saw several building tenants, but didn't see anyone of color. The building has residents of color, doesn't it?"

The building manager told us he did have a tenant of color. We were about to tell him we would take the apartment when he told us he wasn't interested in having us as tenants.

*****

One of the things I've always respected about Russ is his willingness to do the right thing. But that day, I was disappointed. Because of his question, we'd lost the apartment. Russ was embarrassed. He'd voiced an assumption that there were no people of color in the building and he had been wrong. He apologized to me for losing the apartment.

I share the next detail with shame. I responded, "Russ, we had a place. You asked your question. Now we don't have an apartment. Why don't you go out and find us another place?"

Russ, who was looking sheepish, agreed to find an apartment. As I look back at the episode, I was a total asshole. The apartment superintendent's objective had been to have as few people of color in his building as was legally required. In that neighborhood, having only one tenant of color in a building with dozens of residents—well, that wasn't an accident. Russ had had the instincts—the integrity—to ask the right question.

*****

Within a day, Russ had found a basement two-bedroom apartment for ninety dollars a month. While it did not have a view—except for window wells—it was in decent shape. The building's other residents were a mixture of young hip people and older working-class folk—of diverse colors and backgrounds.

We moved into the apartment that day. Any question about the neighborhood being dangerous was quickly resolved. In our first three days in the apartment, police and fire tactical squads arrived twice at our building—with rifles drawn. In both instances, they were responding to phone calls reporting a shoot-out in the building. Both reports turned out to be false alarms.

But we had received official notice. The area was, in fact, tough.

10—Working in the Motor City

The apartment came with twin beds, a few kitchen chairs and a small kitchen table. That first day, we traveled to the local Goodwill Store where we bought pans, dishes, bedding, towels and other basic housekeeping stuff. We also took a city bus to make a big grocery run, carrying the groceries back to our apartment in our backpacks.

*****

It was time to focus on finding jobs. Neither of us qualified for unemployment compensation. But the State of Michigan offered job search services to all unemployed workers. Many companies, including those in the auto industry, used the state unemployment office to screen potential hires. If an unemployed worker was referred by the state to a hiring company, they'd get interviewed, but not necessarily hired.

After learning that I had a college degree, my employment counselor could not understand why I wanted a manual labor position. She told me, "A blue-collar job's going to pay less than a white-collar job and it won't offer you anywhere near the same career path. You ought to be applying management trainee or office worker positions."

I patiently explained to her I wanted to make a living with my hands and body rather than my mind.

She felt that made no sense. But she finally gave up on trying to convince me, saying with a sigh, "OK. You'll be contacted by mail if you get referred for a position."

*****

Over these years, I ran into this a lot. Much of America respected white-collar workers more than blue-collar workers and managers were valued more than line staff. An American myth connected shirts, ties and clean hands with value—and with success.

*****

Detroit businesses did not advertise low wage job openings. They just hired from the stream of applicants who constantly showed up at their offices seeking employment. Russ and I went door-to-door to prospective employers, asking if they had any openings.

Russ found success before I did. He was hired as a swing-shift janitor at Detroit Children's Hospital. His duties were to clean and wax floors, empty trash baskets, vacuum rugs and clean surgery rooms. It was menial work, but Russ liked it. He found it peaceful—and it paid well—two and a half dollars per hour.

Russ told me there were openings on his crew. The next day I went into the Detroit Children's human resources office to apply for a maintenance position. It told them that my friend worked there, liked the work and said I'd worked as a janitor in college—which was technically true. I just hadn't worked at it very hard. Once the interviewer heard I had a college education, she asked why I was not seeking a professional position.

I lied. "I intend to enter graduate school and get a master's degree. This job would pay my expenses while I get a degree."

I could see the relief on her face. It made sense to her that I was deferring power, wealth and prestige until I had a post-graduate degree that would lead to even greater power, wealth and prestige. I had found the succinct explanation that allowed an interviewer to accept my desire to do manual labor.

She hired me.

*****

That position was the best paying job I'd ever had and I liked working the swing-shift. It allowed me to spend my daylight hours as I wished.

On my first day of work, I followed an experienced janitor and learned how to run a large floor polishing, waxing, and buffing machine so that it glided smoothly across the floor. The trick to operating those heavy spinning disk machines is to use a gentle touch. If you push too hard on the machine's handle, the floor polisher ends up caroming off of walls and furniture as if it were a pinball.

One of our responsibilities was cleaning surgery rooms. We made sure they were perfectly sterile so that a room's next young patient was safe from infection. Just hours before I would clean a room, surgeons had performed lifesaving procedures on some small child. As I cleaned and sterilized, I could only imagine the intense circumstances that had resulted in blood being splattered throughout the room.

Within a week, I was comfortable with my new job responsibilities. The work took concentration and focus, but wasn't too difficult.

*****

All janitorial staff took their meals and breaks at the same time in the hospital's huge staff cafeteria. We would troop up to the cafeteria, purchase our coffee and dinner or snack, and sit down at one of the dining hall's tables to eat and drink. Afterwards, we would smoke a cigarette, chat and then return to work.

In the 1970s, it was totally cool to smoke cigarettes. It would've seemed outlandish not to have allowed cigarettes in a dining hall or break room. I knew that smoking could affect my wind. But I didn't know that smoking could kill me. Russ and I each smoked about three cigarettes a day. We tended to borrow or bum cigarettes off of others rather than buy them ourselves. Not only was this a low cost means of funding smoking, but asking for a cigarette was an excellent way to introduce myself to an attractive female employee—not that that ever produced any results other than a cigarette.

*****

A couple of weeks after starting at Children's, I received a postcard from the state employment office. I had been referred for an interview at the Chrysler Assembly Plant in Hamtramck. I went to the interview. The interviewer wasted no time asking about my qualifications or background. He just wanted to identifying any specific issues that would disqualify me. Was I a felon? Was I healthy? Did I have a high school education?

I wasn't disqualified. After a brief physical examination, I was offered a union position with wages of more than five dollars an hour plus benefits.

I was to report for work the following Monday.

*****

I had been working at Children's Hospital for only a couple of weeks. I had been treated with respect and enjoyed my co-workers. But the position with Chrysler paid more than twice as much as Children's. I gave Children's Hospital two days' notice.

I realize now that such short notice was not fair. I hadn't liked it when I wasn't given notice by Max in Portland. At Dockery Lumber Company, a two-week notice hadn't been necessary because of the winter slowdown. And, after my experience on my last day driving a taxi, I'm sure the cab company didn't expect much notice. Still, as I share these experiences, I am not proud of how disrespectful I was to some of my employers.

*****

I'd been in Detroit for less than two months and was about to begin working for an auto manufacturer receiving the highest level of wages I'd ever earned. While I'd start out taking a city bus on the three-mile commute to work, I figured I'd probably end up buying a car. I started to think about staying in Detroit on a long-term basis.

A couple of days after I was hired by Chrysler, Russ received a postcard from the state unemployment office inviting him to interview for a position as a shipping dock supervisor. He was interviewed and took the position. Russ would earn more than four dollars an hour.

We celebrated our upcoming wealth by going out to dinner in Detroit's Greek Town, a neat old neighborhood with wonderful inexpensive Greek restaurants. We ate a fantastic meal of dolmades, moussaka, and souvlaki which we washed down with a bottle of retsina.

*****

My first shift at the Chrysler auto plant started out with a three-hour new employee orientation. I was one of thirty-five new hires who started at Hamtramck that Monday. After a Chrysler human resources representative completed a boring presentation on safety, selecting a health plan and paying union dues, we were photographed for our identification card and ready to go.

The final step in employee orientation was a tour of the factory. We had been informed that Chrysler Hamtramck was the largest automobile factory in the world. None of us doubted that after the tour. Our guide showed us lunch rooms, break rooms, medical services rooms, management offices, bathrooms and an assortment of long and terribly noisy assembly-lines.

There were assembly-lines where vehicle frames were bolted, welded and assembled; lines where engines and power trains were lowered and secured onto automobile frames; others where car seats were attached to vehicle frames; and lines where the outer shell of cars were dropped on top of, then bolted onto, completed automobile frames. There were rooms where car bodies were painted and other rooms where those car shells, wet with paint, were baked to achieve that hard, smooth and shiny finish we all admire on a new car. The assembly-lines—and all the noise they created—went on and on and on.

After the tour, each newly hired Chrysler employee was given a work assignment. At the end of the training, each person would be taken to their new work station. We were warned to pay a lot of attention to the route used to get to that new job location. It was, we were told, easy to get lost in the automobile plant. Until we were familiar with the factory, we were advised to arrive at work early—in case we got lost in the automobile plant.

Fat chance of getting lost inside your place of work, right?

*****

I was now an automobile worker, a member of the United Automobile, Aerospace and Agricultural Implement Workers of America—the UAW. While I had no relevant skills and knew less about building or repairing an automobile than almost anyone else in the whole building, Chrysler had determined that the best role for me would be as a quality control inspector.

Hmmm.

I was taken onto the floor of the factory to my new job station where I met my supervisor. My work station was about eighty yards from the end of the plant's final assembly-line. My supervisor explained to me that as each car came down the assembly-line, I had fifty seconds to walk around it; draw a circle with a large crayon on each imperfection in the car's paint; mark any doors, hoods or trunks not squarely attached to the vehicle—in addition to any other imperfections on the exterior of the car including, but not limited to, body parts that had not been properly painted. During those fifty seconds, I also had to check all engine, radiator and transmission fluid levels. When fluids were below prescribed levels, I had to top them off.

After completing my review of each vehicle, I needed to check off appropriate boxes on a tracking form and sign it. Signing, of course, establishes accountability and we all know that accountability is the cornerstone of quality. After confirming in writing that I had checked everything on the moving car, my fifty seconds ended—and it was time to repeat the process for the next vehicle that was coming down the assembly-line.

It took my supervisor about ten minutes to show me how to do my job. Then, I was on my own. Quality control had never been so assured!

*****

From the late 1940s to the early 1970s, CBS Television had a Sunday night variety program called *The Ed Sullivan Show*. Ed often had a guest named Erich Brenn who spun plates on sticks. Ed's audience would gasp as Brenn rushed from stick to stick speeding up spinning plates so that none would fall to the floor and break. My new job seemed a lot like the work done by Mr. Brenn. To make my quality control procedures even more similar to Brenn's spinning plates on sticks, I had to complete all of my inspections steps while almost assembled vehicles were slowly creeping past me on an assembly-line.

*****

In 1910, Chrysler's Hamtramck plant was built by the Dodge Brothers and called Dodge Main. It took the name Chrysler Hamtramck (after the Hamtramck suburb in which it was located) in the 1920s when Chrysler bought Dodge. The building was a hodge-podge combination of nine individual, now connected, buildings. While the factory had been updated and restructured often during its sixty years, its fundamental structure hadn't changed much since 1910. I recently saw a photograph of plant operations from 1918. With the primary exception of the vintage of automobiles on the line, it looked a lot like the factory where I worked.

Being there was an intense experience that merged motion, activity and noise. The assembly line was a river of chrome, wheels, glass and painted steel. Each of its thousands of employees performed unique tasks in the assembly of diverse Chrysler, Dodge and Plymouth cars. When an automobile was complete, I inspected it to make sure that Chrysler's standard of quality had been successfully achieved.

Everyone at the plant worked intensely. There was no need or opportunity for small talk. Since the racket in the factory was so great, if I had to speak with another person, I had to yell.

*****

During my first shift, I immediately recognized the intense focus required—and I did the best I could. But, about two or three hours after I started, a supervisor from further down the line came up to me and said, "I need to show you something."

He led me to a vehicle I had inspected ten minutes earlier. He showed me my signature on its quality review form. Vehicles continued to move down the line as he took me to the back of that car and showed me an area underneath the bumper where the body of the car had not received its final coat of paint. It only had been primed—and I had not marked it.

He said, "This is the type of error you can't make. If this sort of shit continues to get past you, you're gonna be fired." Then, he allowed me to return to my station. During the time he had spoken with me, five cars had passed my station without any quality control inspection.

So, it goes.

*****

During my lunch break, I ate my peanut butter and jelly sandwiches, drank my coffee and smoked a cigarette. The intensity of the factory had left me without any energy or desire to chat with co-workers. When the half-hour break ended, I returned to my station and relieved the worker who had stood in for me during my lunch. I was back to the never-ending flow of Chryslers, noise, and details that needed inspection to assure quality.

*****

The paint baking room was like a large oven containing multiple vehicles that had just been sprayed with paint. The intense heat baked the wet paint onto the cars' bodies. During that first shift, a commotion occurred on the far side of the plant near the vehicle paint baking room. I learned later that the room's sliding door had been shut and its ovens turned on while a worker was still in the room. Factory workers realized there was a problem when they saw an oil residue in the stream of water that flowed out of the paint baking room. That oil residue was melted fat from the body of the deceased worker.

*****

I watched the clock closely that first evening. Orientation and learning my job had exhausted me. I couldn't wait for my eight-hour shift to end.

But about an hour before my shift was due to end, I was informed that we would be working three hours of overtime. I would earn about thirty dollars in those three hours—an incredible amount! But I was tired. I wanted to go home.

I left the plant at three in the morning and headed out of the factory to take the bus home. That was when I learned there were no public buses at that hour of the morning. I walked the three miles home arriving at around four-thirty in the morning at my apartment. I was exhausted and fell into bed. I was immediately was transported, via a dream, back to the assembly-line. Vehicles moved past me in my sleep—a continuation of the noise and dizzying activity of the prior evening.

*****

I woke up more tired than I had been when I went to bed. After a large breakfast, I caught a bus and arrived at the factory fifteen minutes early. I wanted to be certain I was at my station on the factory floor before my shift started.

The factory seemed larger than I remembered. Fifteen minutes turned out to be an insufficient amount of time to find my work station. I arrived at it ten minutes late. My supervisor greeted me by saying, "If you want to keep this job, never let this happen again."

I had worked at Hamtramck for a little over one shift and had been told twice that I had one more chance before I would be fired.

This job was going to be a piece of cake.

*****

My second shift at Chrysler Hamtramck was much the same as my first. The procession of new cars requiring flaw identification and engine fluid was unending. But I began to get the rhythm of the job and was able to relax a little.

I chatted with some of my co-workers during coffee and meal breaks. None of those I spoke with felt that Chrysler valued them as human beings. They were simply extensions of machinery. Without exception, they hated the assembly-line, but needed the money. Most of them got through their shift by focusing on how they would spend their earnings—on new cars, fast boats, bigger houses—or paying for their kids' educations. There was always one more large purchase that justified staying rather than moving on to a more humane job.

That evening, we had to work overtime again. For the second night in a row, I walked back to my apartment in the middle of the night. I was exhausted when I climbed into bed and once more dreamt non-stop of the assembly-line. When I awoke, it was clear to me that if I was going to continue at Hamtramck, I needed to buy a car.

*****

My third shift was similar to my second with the exception that I did not get lost in the factory on the way to my station. I was not quite as tired at the end of that eleven-hour shift. But when I finally got into bed and went to sleep, my dreams were just as unpleasant as they had been on the prior two nights.

I was not enjoying the auto industry.

*****

As I started my fourth shift, I was already exhausted from long and intense work days, three-mile walks home and poor nights' sleep dominated by assembly-line dreams. I was so tired that the job didn't seem worth it. During my lunch hour, I told my supervisor that it wasn't working out—I wanted to quit. He told me he wanted me to talk to the floor manager and led me to a man with a tie and white shirt—a uniform that indicated this man was in a power position.

The floor manager told me he wanted me to reconsider. "We've had our eye on you. It's rare that we get a college graduate in here who's willing to work on the floor and knows how to work hard. In addition, the quality of your work is pretty good. Why don't you go home, rest today and Friday; then on Monday morning, let us start you off on a white-collar job?"

The offer was generous. But I was tired and disgusted with how things were being managed at the auto plant. I told him, "I don't think so. At this point, if I never work for any auto industry related company again, it'll be too soon. I appreciate the offer, but I'm done."

I filled out my resignation form, left the factory, and because it wasn't the middle of the night, I was able to catch a bus home.

*****

I had learned a lesson: The best paying job may not be the best job to accept. How one is treated on a job is more important than how much one earns. As I look back at my time working in an automobile assembly plant, I think of the Charlie Chaplin film *Modern Times* and appreciate how well it describes how factory workers are dehumanized.

*****

A couple of days later, I started looking for my next job. While on the search, I had lunch at a pizza restaurant near Wayne State University. The restaurant had a sign in its window: *Pizza Chef Wanted*. I walked up to a woman at the cash register and asked her about the opening. She looked over her shoulder at a man who was working behind her, intently making pizzas. I spoke to him. His name was Tony and he was the owner. Tony invited me to sit down with him at one of the restaurant's tables. He asked about my experience as a cook.

I was honest. "I've never been a cook. But I've been a waiter—and a busboy."

Evidently those were exactly the qualifications I needed. Without any other questions, I was hired. If his lack of questions didn't set off any alarms, then the fact that he asked me to start work immediately should have. I finished the piece of pizza I had already purchased, put on a pizza chef apron and—presto—I was Tony's new pizza chef.

Tony was in his early forties. He was a hustler, a successful small business entrepreneur who pushed himself and other people to produce more with less. Tony owned several small restaurants in Detroit. He didn't overpay or baby his staff—we were paid the minimum wage of $1.60 an hour and worked a six-hour shift, five days a week—not a ton of money—but, because I was sharing housing expenses with Russ, it was enough to get by. The only employee benefit was free lunches at work.

*****

Tony spent an hour and a half showing me the ropes. I learned how to turn a handful of dough into a pizza crust; how to shred ten-pound blocks of mozzarella cheese; and how to set up fresh and canned condiments and meats that ended up on the pizzas. Tony explained the routines for heating up canned soup and for chopping lettuce. No dishwashing was involved. We used disposable plates, plastic silverware and paper cups.

My co-worker was a young woman named Patricia. She helped me set up in the morning, kept the tables cleared during lunch hour and ran the cash register. Tony stopped by and checked in at the restaurant once every couple of days—always taking the time to tell us what we were doing wrong.

My daily routine at the restaurant began at ten in the morning. Once I had unlocked the restaurant and put on my long white apron, I turned on the pizza oven, opened a two gallon can of minestrone soup and heated up its contents. Then I cut up vegetable condiments, shredded the mozzarella, set out the meats, and got everything ready for the lunch hour. At 11:30, I opened the front door to the public and presto, I was no longer Roger, the set-up guy. I had become Roger, the pizza chef.

*****

I liked making pizzas. It was fun rolling out the dough, throwing those flat ovals into the air, catching them on my fists and stretching them out. Once the thin flat pizza dough was placed onto a large oval pan, I added a lot of sauce, didn't skimp on the cheese and included plenty of sliced vegetables, Italian sausage and pepperoni.

Tony had told me to be sparing with food ingredients. "They are expensive."

But I ignored his direction and made good pizzas. Our customers liked pizzas the way I made them—and told me so. I probably used fifteen percent more ingredients than I was supposed to use. So, each pizza probably cost twenty-five cents more than Tony would have preferred. But people came back to the restaurant because they liked the pizza. That seemed like a fairly decent reward for a small increase in cost.

The restaurant was close enough to Wayne State University that our clientele included a lot of students. Other customers worked for local businesses. Many of our regulars seemed like interesting folk. It was satisfying when they thanked me for preparing such a good pizza.

When Tony came into the restaurant, he would always yell at Patricia or me. He explained that it wasn't personal—it was his management style. I quickly learned to ignore Tony—that was my employee style. Patricia and I got along well. Our conversations focused on making sure everything was prepared for the next customer and, when Tony wasn't there, commenting on what a creep he was.

*****

I had worked at Tony's for a little over a week when one day, as I set up for lunch, I left a large stainless-steel spoon in the minestrone as it was heating. When I grabbed the spoon to stir the soup, I confirmed the theory that steel is an excellent conductor of heat. My hand was burned badly. I immediately looked for the first aid kit. That was when I learned the restaurant did not have a first aid kit. I walked down the street to a corner drugstore and bought some ointment and a bandage. I was back at the restaurant within five minutes and sat down at a table with a glass of ice water. Big, ugly, bright pink blisters were already forming across my hand where it had had been in contact with the hot spoon. I put the ointment and bandage I had purchased onto my hand.

The accident had been my fault. But no first aid kit and no opportunity for me to take time off to treat my injured hand were issues that bothered me. Tony came into the restaurant while I was at the drugstore. When I returned, he showed no interest in my burn. But about a couple minutes after I had returned from the drugstore, he said, "Well, are you coming back to work or not?"

I looked at him, paused for a moment, considering the pros and cons of alternative responses. Even though I enjoyed making pizzas, Tony's big mouth and lack of tact had gotten under my skin.

I responded, "No Tony. I'm not coming back. I quit."

I took off my apron, handed it to him, informed him I would pick up my final paycheck on payday and walked out.

And with that, my career as a pizza chef ended and I had learned why Tony had difficulty retaining pizza chefs.

*****

Meanwhile, Russ was enjoying his job with the shipping company. Management liked him and he got along well with the union workers that loaded and unloaded trucks. His tenure at the trucking company was the longest either of us had had a job in Detroit. However, a few days after I left the pizza restaurant, Russ faced a difficult issue. His manager told him the trucking company had to lay off one of their loading dock supervisors. The company was going to lay off the other supervisor, even though that man had been with the company a lot longer than Russ.

Russ had gotten to know the other dock supervisor. He had a family, appeared to be a conscientious worker, had much more seniority and was doing a good job. But Russ had a good idea why his co-worker was being laid off. He was black.

Russ always has done and always will do what he considers to be the right thing. He told his manager he was quitting—they could retain the other dock supervisor. So, a day or two after I left the pizza restaurant, we were both unemployed.

*****

It was late October 1972. Russ and I had been in Detroit for about two months. And neither of us had a job.

11—Amazing Grace

Russ and I were both looking for a similar unskilled labor position. For that reason, on a sunny Monday in November, he and I started separate job searches at opposite ends of Detroit's primary business corridor. I began in downtown Detroit and headed north along Woodward Avenue. Russ started four miles to the north and headed south on Woodward.

Sounds like a good approach, right?

*****

When I applied for jobs in Detroit, I ran into consistent patterns from prospective employers. After entering a business's office, I asked the receptionist, "Who can I speak with about job openings?"

The receptionist was almost always a woman. She told me there were no openings. I'd ask her if I could fill out an application anyway. She generally said something like, "We just aren't taking applications at this time."

But sometimes, she would give me an application form. I would take five to ten minutes filling it out, then I'd hand the competed form to the receptionist.

She would say, "Thank you. We will contact you if there are any openings."

But sometimes, she would take the application into a back office and return a moment later saying, "Your application is being reviewed."

In those instances, a person who was senior to the receptionist would come out of an office a few minutes later. He or she would whisper something to the receptionist who would say, "We will contact you if any openings come up," or she would say, "Mr. Smith would like to speak with you about your application."

When Mr. Smith, Miss Smith or whatever the HR specialist's name was, came out from their cubicle, they would invite me into an interview room and ask several questions—including of course, "Why are you applying for a low-tier position when you have a college degree?"

After we had discussed my master's degree plans, they would become noticeably more at ease and tell me about any openings. All of this, of course, is now streamlined and automated. But during my odyssey, it took persistence, politeness and luck.

And as an aside, it was interesting that in a city like Detroit—which was predominantly populated by people of color—I met no interviewers who were persons of color.

*****

That particular morning, I had been persistent. I had been polite. But I hadn't been lucky. At midday, I walked into the human resources office for Grace Hospital, a large, central Detroit healthcare facility. I was surprised. Russ was sitting there, filling out some form. Then it occurred to me that Grace Hospital was in the middle of our routes. We each had already covered half of Woodward Avenue's businesses.

I walked up to the receptionist, told her I was looking for a lower-level position and asked if they had any openings. She politely told me that they had no openings but I could fill out an application if I wished. I took the application, sat down, filled it out and returned it to her. She informed me that the hospital would contact me if any openings came up.

Russ was filling out a second form. I asked him what it was. He told me it was some sort of aptitude test. He said it was pretty interesting. So, I walked up to the receptionist and asked her if I could take the same test my friend was taking.

She said "Sure" and handed me a brief multiple-choice questionnaire on a clipboard.

Filling out the questionnaire was a fun distraction after a long and tedious morning. While I worked on it, Russ handed her his completed form. Several minutes later, he was asked to go into a backroom for an interview. I didn't pay much attention to what Russ was doing. I was intrigued with the game-like questions on what amounted to an aptitude test. When I finished filling it out, I handed it to the receptionist. She asked me to take a chair.

While I waited, Russ came out of his interview and gave me a double thumbs up. In order to try to remain somewhat discrete, I didn't chat with him about what that meant. Several minutes later, the receptionist called back to the woman who had interviewed Russ. I heard the receptionist say, "Martha, we've got another brilliant one."

*****

A few minutes later, I was asked to speak with the woman who had interviewed Russ. I followed her into a small office. She asked me a few of the usual questions about myself including what sort of job I wanted and what my long-term plans were. I had my responses pretty well nailed down—I wanted a basic job that would allow me to go to grad school so I could cover my living and tuition expenses.

The interviewer told me the hospital had two vacant orderly positions. She explained that orderlies worked as a pool for all areas within the hospital and described their duties. The job paid almost three dollars an hour and included benefits. She told me she had just offered one position to Russ. Then she offered me the other.

I was thrilled. I told her the job seemed perfect. We chatted for a few minutes about my other work experiences. As I described my jobs since college, she came to realize that I might not turn into a long-term employee. At one point during this conversation, she laughed and said, "I am not certain why I just hired you!"

I was relieved that her comment was made in jest. I still had the job.

*****

Then the interviewer asked Russ to join us. She shared more information about the positions. One of them worked a day-shift starting at seven in the morning. The other worked the night-shift and began at 11 PM. Russ asked me if it was okay if he took the day-shift. It would allow him to work with professional staff on complex medical procedures. Since Russ would be studying medicine, the knowledge and experience he gained would be useful to him.

We filled out a couple of additional forms and were told to start work in two days. An hour later, we were enjoying a lunch in a small restaurant, celebrating our successful employment search.

*****

Getting from our apartment to Grace Hospital was easy. Our apartment was two blocks from the bus line. Grace hospital was that same distance from the same bus line.

On my first day at Grace, I reported to the orderlies' room on the hospital ground floor. It was adjacent to the emergency room and had an interior window that looked out at the emergency room's entrance. On one end of the room near the window, it was furnished with a supervisor's desk and chair. Along the other walls of the room, there were seven or eight banquet chairs.

My new supervisor, Otis, was a black man of medium height and build with a modest Afro haircut. He welcomed me to the hospital, then introduced me to the other orderlies. The orderly I remember most clearly, was Solomon Smith. Solomon was a small wiry man in his fifties. He had short graying hair, a short, neatly trimmed mustache and a soul patch under his bottom lip. Otis and the orderlies were all dressed in blue medical scrubs—an outfit I would also wear.

Otis invited me to sit down on a chair next to his desk. He started out with, "Probably, the first thing we need to do is to review our list of rules."

Then he proceeded to briefly open and examine each drawer of his desk looking for those rules. I waited patiently. Finally, Otis lifted his desktop pad, checking underneath it (in case the rules had been somehow hidden there). When list of rules wasn't there, he said, "Well, I guess we'll just have to go over the rules some other day."

There were no set of written rules. Otis was just having fun with me. I had been introduced to Otis' warm demeanor which was the cornerstone of my new and pretty awesome job. And that was not the last time I was slow on catching the nuanced humor of my co-workers at Grace Hospital.

*****

After ending his search for the phantom list of rules, Otis detailed the duties of Grace Hospital orderlies. We were at the beck and call of nurses throughout the hospital. They would call us whenever they needed assistance. That might be support in managing an aggressive patient; help lifting something; moving a patient from one area to another; transporting the body of a deceased person to the hospital morgue; bathing a male patient; or giving a man an enema.

Any time a hospital station needed support from the orderlies, a phone call was made to the orderlies' room. Otis took the call and assigned one of us to respond. We were sent out on a rotating basis and workloads were managed so that each of us ended up doing a similar amount of work. While his style was laid-back, Otis had the trust and respect of all hospital employees and took great pride in the professionalism of those who worked for him. We understood that the quality with which we performed our tasks made a difference to patients and other hospital staff.

*****

Hospitals in the inner city of Detroit worked in collaboration with one another. Each hospital had an area of focus. Grace was the primary emergency room and trauma center for the city and provided services to those who sought emergency care for severe diseases, heart attacks and auto accidents. Some of our patients were victims of gun shots and knifings. Some had had drug overdoses. Others had attempted to commit suicide. We were even the primary emergency room for auto industry employees injured at work in Detroit's automobile factories.

In addition to providing initial hospital care to those who came in for emergency treatment, Grace provided specialty care for adults who had severe cases of cancer and other life-threatening chronic diseases.

*****

That first night, Otis gave me a tour of the hospital and introduced me to the many nurses, housekeeping and specialty staff who worked the night-shift. It was abundantly clear how much everyone I met cared for and respected Otis. But during this tour, I also came to realize that Grace Hospital was a place where all staff not only took great pride in their work, but always treated one another in a respectful and gracious manner.

I was warmly welcomed by each hospital employee. But I quickly noticed that with the exception of the retired police officer who served as a security guard next to the emergency room, I was the only white male working the night-shift at Grace Hospital.

The people I worked with were extremely professional. The service they delivered to their patients was driven by a work culture that took pride in quality. The level of teamwork between staff within the hospital amazed me. And what was even more amazing was that there was no training on teamwork. Teamwork and respect for one another were the bedrock of the hospital's culture, not an add-on learned behavior.

*****

For the first couple of nights, I tagged along behind other orderlies on service calls throughout the hospital. Within a week, I had learned the required techniques and routines well enough to provide a full array of services without assistance from another orderly. Work was fascinating because I could never anticipate what sort of emergent situation might require my next response.

When a nurse had a particularly heavy patient, I assisted her in moving the patient from a gurney to a bed or in changing his or her bedding. Sometimes that sort of task was routine. Other times, it became an intense challenge.

Another orderly and I were once sent up to a ward to help a nurse change the bedding for a patient who weighed over four hundred pounds. Because of serious heart and weight issues, the patient was not able to move out of or around on his bed. The other orderly and I helped the patient, a young man who was probably not more than thirty years old, onto his right side while the nurse rolled up the bedding on the other half of the mattress to replace it with fresh bedding. While we were holding the patient on his right side, he began to roll forward off the bed. He was so large and so difficult to grasp, that it took all of our strength to prevent him from falling off the bed. A third orderly was called to assist us so that the nurse could finish changing the bedding.

*****

While waiting for requests for service, we sat in the orderlies' room and shot the shit while listening to rhythm and blues played by a local AM radio station. Some of our conversations amounted to small talk. At other times, a co-worker would share personal memories. For me, those shared stories were the most special part of working at Grace Hospital.

In particular, Solomon Smith's accounts from his life were joyful—almost always either hilarious or fascinating—and often both. They included memories of growing up in Alabama, stories about his misfortunes serving in the military in Korea, accounts of drunken nights out on the town and brief anecdotes as simple as an argument with his wife.

Solomon's sophisticated sense of humor, incredible sense of timing, and ability to keep a straight face while we howled with laughter made him a master storyteller. His colorful use of language added dimension to his stories. I loved his description of January's cold Detroit weather as *the hawk is biting now*.

When Solomon started telling a tale, everyone was riveted. Once he had us laughing intensely, he would pause and say, "To make a long story short." He would wait, straight faced, for a few seconds until we gained control over our laughter, and then repeat "to make a long story short" again and again as a means of making his stories longer— and making his co-workers laugh harder.

*****

Solomon once shared a beautiful memory of his childhood. He told us about his extended family's barbecues in the late 1930s. Solomon Smith had been raised on a small family farm in Alabama. On hot Saturdays in the summer, his parents, brothers, sisters, aunts, uncles, cousins and the family's close neighbors and friends would get together for a softball game and barbecue.

Several days before the barbecue, the men folk would dig a pit several feet deep. They would start a fire in the pit using large pieces of hickory. Then they slaughtered and gutted a goat, slathered it with homemade barbecue sauce made from brown sugar, vinegar, tomato sauce and spices. They wrapped the goat in burlap that had also been thoroughly soaked with the barbecue sauce. When the burning hickory turned into a bed of coals, they placed the wrapped and dressed goat carcass onto the coals. Then they covered the pit with hickory branches and filled it in with soil.

As Solomon described it, the day of the barbecue was a large extended family celebration. The kids and men would play a softball game. Afterwards, they would dig up the barbecued goat and serve it with coleslaw, fresh squeezed lemonade and whatever potluck dishes family members brought.

After Solomon finished sharing this thirty-five-year-old memory, it seemed like I had been at the barbeque and had experienced the warmth and joy of his extended family. I felt as if the hot sun at the ball game had burned my shoulders. I could almost smell the tender barbecued goat. And I wanted some of that that freshly squeezed lemonade!

*****

The laughter we enjoyed in the orderlies' room was interspersed with moments of intense attention to work. We had many patients who were close to death. Often times, when we were moving a patient on a gurney or providing some other service, the patient's level of pain was extraordinary. Some of those people were very sad. They had good reason. Their lives had become hard. One of our responsibilities as an orderly was to treat our patients with respect.

There was one older man who was so angry about his illness that he treated everyone with disrespect. As his condition worsened, he only became more bitter. I remember cleaning him up in his bed as he cursed me along with every other staff person in the hospital. I still treated him with respect.

Three hours later, I was moving his body down to the morgue.

*****

At the same time that an orderly was notified to transport a deceased person to the morgue, a doctor was notified that he or she needed to speak with the deceased person's family. Only then was the family called. When the family arrived at the hospital, the doctor would speak with them, telling them that their loved one had passed away and responding to their questions and needs.

I was moving a deceased patient's body from his hospital room to the morgue. Protocol had been followed. The nurse had communicated with the doctor before calling the family. But the son and daughter had been en route to the hospital when their father had passed. As I was beginning to move the body on a gurney to the morgue, the family arrived in the cancer ward. I was wheeling the patient out of the hospital room, covered with a sheet on the gurney, when a nurse ran up to me and said the family was walking down the hall toward me. I immediately turned around and took the patient back into the hospital room.

The deceased man's son and daughter opened the door to the hospital room and asked me, as I stood in the doorway, how their father was doing. I told them, "The doctor is coming to speak with you."

They pleaded. "But you can tell us, can't you? Is our father alive? You need to be able to tell us this. Can't you please help us?"

How powerless I felt! I responded again that I was not able to say more. It would've been inappropriate for me to tell them that their father had died. If one of them had reacted strongly to that information, I didn't have the skills to respond. But my heart went out to the family as I wondered where the hell the doctor was.

Eventually, a nurse came to my rescue and led the family to a conference room to meet with the doctor (who still had not arrived). I quickly moved the deceased patient down the hall—away from the family—and into the morgue.

*****

At times, the emergency room seemed like a war zone. Seriously injured auto workers would arrive by ambulance from the auto factories. One young man had taken drugs before going to work. A rivet had been driven through his hand while he used an assembly-line tool. The young man was so high on drugs he could not feel the pain.

Another patient had suffered a serious head injury in a car accident. The emergency room was extremely busy and there were no nurses available to assist the doctor as he dressed the wound. The injured man had lost so much blood that the doctor was unable to administer a pain killer. I was asked to assist the doctor. I spoke to the injured man and held his shoulders—keeping him from moving—while the doctor cleansed his wound, examined his skull and sealed his scalp with stitches. At one point, the doctor said, "Let me show you something." He moved aside the skin by the scalp wound and showed me a crack in the man's skull.

*****

Each morning, my shift ended at seven. I generally got home from work a little before eight and then went to bed. While I often slept for six or seven hours, sometimes I would get up after three or four hours of sleep to take better advantage of the daylight hours. On days off, I would revert to a schedule of sleeping at night. Due to this inconsistent sleep schedule, I was often groggy.

One morning on my way home from work, a squad car pulled up to me as I stepped off the city bus. The policeman got out of his car, walked up to me and said in an intimidating manner, "Where are you coming from?"

I'd been working all night and had been tired even before getting to work. The officer's intense tone threw me off. I blanked out. I told him that I couldn't remember where

I'd been. He followed up quickly by asking me for my name and address. I began to panic. I couldn't even remember my name! Finally, the officer asked to see my identification. I took a deep breath, pulled out my wallet and showed him my driver's license and Grace Hospital identification.

I began to regained composure and said, "Look, I've been working all night at Grace Hospital and I'm really tired."

He accepted that and told me to go home and get some sleep.

I know that being a cop is a dangerous job. Those of us who have never served on a police force have no idea of the pressures, dangers and responsibilities that are a part of each day for law enforcement officers. But as in most American cities, black people in Detroit were generally targeted by the police more often than those who were white. However, there were some white people who also appeared to get targeted and it seems like I was one of them.

Another morning as I left work, I boarded the bus at my usual bus stop. A moment later a police car came racing down Woodward Avenue with its siren howling and lights flashing. The bus moved over to the side of the road as the squad car pulled over, at an angle, in front of the bus. Two police officers got out of the squad car with guns drawn. One of the officers boarded the bus from the front door; the other officer boarded the bus behind me from the rear door. They converged on me with guns drawn. One of them tensely asked, "Where have you been? Show us some identification."

I had never been interrogated with one gun pointed at me. Now, there were two of them. I took the officers very seriously, explaining to them that I'd been at work at Grace

Hospital and showing them my driver's license and hospital identification. They put their guns back into their holsters and explained that a robbery had taken place in an area near where I had boarded the bus. They had thought I was the perpetrator.

My co-workers told me that the police force in Detroit was primarily white and often pretty aggressive. A neighbor of a co-worker, a young black man, had been in his backyard when a squad car drove down his alley. A police officer in the squad car spotted the young man and questioned him. The cops must not have liked his responses because they beat him up. The young man ended up seriously injured, spending a week in a hospital bed. I don't know what the young man said to the cops, but the beating served no purpose. I was told that this sort of violence was not unusual.

I had one other episode with the Detroit police. I was walking along the sidewalk near our apartment when a squad car pulled up. The officers got out of the car and approached me. They had me lean forward spread eagle with my hands on the front of the police car. I assume the reason they patted me down was to make sure I had no weapons. They asked me a few questions, then let me go. The only reason I can think of for their targeting me was because I had long hair.

*****

Two of my more interesting co-workers were both named Robert. Big Robert and Little Robert were orderlies on the dayshift. Big Robert was not actually that big. Nor was he overweight or tall. He was called Big Robert to distinguish him from Little Robert who was quite petite.

Big Robert was a confident character who had had many different occupations and had lived in many different parts of the world. Big Robert was a great story teller who often enriched his facts to make his stories even more fascinating.

One morning, Big Robert came into the orderlies' room shortly before the end of our night-shift. The Temptations' hit song *Papa was a Rolling Stone* was playing on the radio. The song is a wonderful mélange of narrative and rhythm; the story of a young man who didn't know his recently deceased father very well. The song tells how the young man asked his mother to tell him more about his dad. The young man adds, "And mama, some bad talking going around that papa had three outside children and another wife—and that ain't right".

That morning, as we listened to the song, Big Robert stood in the center of our orderlies' room nodding his head to the rhythm of the music. And then Big Robert began to speak. "I remember when my daddy died. Mama got my brother and sister and me dressed up for the funeral. We went down to the church. While we waited for the service, I saw some of momma's friends. They looked like they'd been crying. And their kids were there too—I'd never seen them before. Each of those kids—they looked like they could've been one of my brothers or sisters".

Robert paused for a moment. He hadn't stopped moving his head softly with the beat, keeping time with the music. He continued. "Daddy used to be away for long times. Mama said that he had a job in another city and that's why we didn't see him. But seeing those kids at the funeral—how much they looked like my brother and sister—well, that caused me to wonder—how well had I known my pop?"

He had narrated that story slowly, in a sad voice that kept pace with the rhythm of the music. At the end of the song, there is a long instrumental. During that instrumental, Robert just continued to keep rhythm with the song, moving his head in time with the beat. When the song ended, Big Robert was silent for a moment. We were all silent. Then, Robert took a deep breath and slowly left the orderlies' room.

I was moved by the story. I sat quietly, feeling a lot of sympathy after hearing the painful account Robert had shared.

Otis looked at me and said, "You didn't believe any of that horseshit, did you?"

What could I say?

Otis and the other orderlies roared with laughter.

*****

Tom Walker was a seventy-year-old retired Detroit police officer. But he was also the hospital's day-shift security guard. Tom was white, slight of build and had short thinning, but carefully groomed gray hair. He had a nice disposition, a great sense of humor and no desire to stand out.

Tom shared a funny story a few days after the day-shift workers had their Christmas party. He told me he had been watching his co-workers dance to rhythm and blues when he saw a young, beautiful black woman whom he didn't recognize. He walked up to her and asked her to dance.

While they were dancing, Tom said, "I don't remember seeing you around. You work at the hospital?"

The petite young woman with very dark skin, long eyelashes and sparkly blue eye shadow responded in a sweet and feminine voice, "Why you know me Mr. Walker. I'm Little Robert."

When Tom told me this story, his face turned a deep crimson and he started laughing. He told me he stopped dancing and quickly stepped away from Little Robert. As a white retired city cop, this whole episode was way out of his comfort zone.

However, Tom Walker had the strength and the sense of humor to laugh at himself.

*****

A large empty lot about ten blocks from my apartment was used as a neighborhood football field. On Saturday afternoons, young adult men in the neighborhood met there to play touch football. I had always enjoyed playing football and joined them five or six times that fall. I was the only white guy on the field. The other players, all from the neighborhood, welcomed me. It probably helped that I had pretty fair skills, could take and deliver a hit and didn't act like an arrogant—and bigoted—white boy.

*****

Throughout college, I had a friend named Karen with whom I was deeply infatuated. From time to time, our friendship would begin to move to the next level; then it would fall back as often happens with intense young people. I continued to write her during my travels in spite of the fact that she was living with another guy.

At Carleton, Karen had introduced me to women's literature. With her strong encouragement, I came to appreciate the sheer genius of Virginia Woolf and several other women writers. I became aware of these writers' worlds of details—feelings, color and texture—that contrasted with the more intellectual, idea-oriented approach to life I had learned from my father.

Karen had been my one great college infatuation. She was passionate, attractive, high strung and highly literate. We worked together as waiters in a student dining hall. After serving meals to students, waiters would sit down together, drink coffee, tell stories and laugh. Her sense of humor and long blonde hair attracted me. I think my shyness gave her a level of comfort. During my senior year, when she became seriously involved with someone else, I was devastated.

I received a letter from Karen. She had broken up with her boyfriend and moved to Chicago—only three hundred miles from me. She asked if she could visit me in Detroit. I was thrilled. Within a week, we had arranged a three-day visit.

The visit went well. Karen and I recalled and cherished good memories. And we chose not to revisit old issues that might have been tough to resolve. We had a lot of fun and my infatuation was rekindled. Russ, who had not known Karen well during college, understood why I was so taken with her. A couple of weeks after Karen came to Detroit, I visited her in Chicago. Again, we had a great time.

*****

I was feeling good about my life. I had a job I liked, lived with a great friend in a neat apartment in a cool city. And to top it off, I was in love with someone who lived only three hundred miles away. What more could I ask for?

*****

One especially sad memory from Grace Hospital is of a young man who came into the emergency room in incredible pain. He was seventeen or eighteen years old and looked totally healthy. But an emergency room nurse explained to me he had sickle cell anemia, a disease that occurs primarily in young black men. The nurse told me he came into the emergency room fairly often.

That first time I saw him in the emergency room, after the pain had subsided, I discovered how soft-spoken and thoughtful he was. In fact, he was one of the gentlest people I'd met during my time in Detroit. The last time I saw him, he was devastated by pain. A few hours later, he passed away—there—in the emergency room.

I had the duty of moving his body to the morgue.

*****

Detroit turned out to be a wonderful city in which to live. When Russ and I first arrived, what stood out was that the city was well past its prime; full of empty homes, boarded up stores and empty offices. The white middle-class had vacated the city. They had moving to the suburbs. And many businesses followed them. But the marvelous architecture, the classic skyscrapers and attractive brick apartment buildings were still there echoing Detroit's importance as the Motor City it had been in its heyday.

The people we met from the black community welcomed us. As time passed, we came to appreciate many aspects of the city including its world class music. Detroit Music in the early seventies was really special. The rest of the country and much of the rest of the world were listening to Motown. Russ bought a component stereo system giving us music in our apartment. I was able to enjoy the Temptations, the Four Tops, Gladys Knight and the Pips, Roberta Flack, Al Greene, Aretha Franklin, and countless other rhythm and blues stars at home as well as at work.

Russ and I were visited by a friend from Carleton College whose undergraduate and postgraduate degrees were in music. During his visit, we got tickets to a concert billed as *The World's Greatest Gospel Show*. It featured the finest gospel singers in the country.

It was a great concert. Our friend from Carleton was inspired. In the years that followed, he focused on documenting gospel music and later became a recognized national authority on that art form.

*****

Traveling by public transit opened our lives to diverse people who lived in Detroit's inner-city. Russ told a wonderful story about one bus ride. As he got onto the bus, he heard a woman reciting the names of movies she wanted to see. There was a rhythm in her words.

"I wanna see Gunfight at the OK Corral—I wanna see Casablanca—I wanna see The Naked City—I want to see Gone with the Wind. I want to see The Day the Earth Stood Still—I wanna see The Blob—I wanna see Public Enemy Number One—I wanna see...."

During that bus ride, the woman continued to recite names of an array of films—all classics—all extraordinarily popular in their time. She did not stop chanting those movies she wanted to see and was still going as he got off the bus twenty minutes later. The amazing thing, Russ noted, was that she did not repeat the title of a single film.

*****

One evening, walking back to our apartment after a satisfying (and inexpensive) dinner, I was singing the song *Moonshadow* by Cat Stevens. As I walked down the street, I saw an album someone had dropped next to the curb. When I picked it up, I saw it was *Teaser and the Firecat*, the album by Cat Stevens that featured *Moonshadow,* the song I had been singing.

That sort of madness or enchantment—I'm not sure which—was the fabric of Detroit that we enjoyed. Living in Detroit was at times like being an actor in a Fellini movie.

*****

One of the most interesting characters we met in Detroit was a woman named Asa. Asa stood out on the street, crying out to whomever would listen about the crimes that had been perpetrated against her. Most people would look at a deranged person like her as a lunatic. They would stay away from her. Russ approached things differently. He went up to her and asked her about herself.

He learned that Asa was originally from Yugoslavia. She had been enslaved in a concentration camp by the Nazis. Nazi guards had raped her repeatedly. Then, as the war ended and the Soviet Union drove the Nazis out of Yugoslavia, Asa was put in an asylum. The abuse she suffered continued. It was just that Asa had become the victim of a different conqueror.

As she stood on the street and proclaimed her anger against the world, Asa gave us hand-written diatribes documenting her pain. Her angry language was imbued with a rhythm that made her rants almost musical. At first, those rants seemed nonsensical. However, once you had heard her account of what she had endured, her outbursts—all of the anger—seemed totally understandable. Asa was not insane—she had been literally and figuratively tortured—by a world that was insane.

Knowing someone who has gone off the deep end like Asa, then learning what caused her behavior, should teach anyone who hasn't experienced that terror to have compassion—not to judge so quickly. Meeting a person like Asa should be a reminder to appreciate the safety and security we so easily take for granted.

*****

A few weeks after my first visit, I hitchhiked to Chicago to visit Karen a second time. The visit started out with laughter, nice walks and conversation. We talked about the possibility of living together. I was unwilling to move from Detroit because I understood how easily I could lose the balance I had found in my life. Karen felt a similar vulnerability. She wanted to live in Chicago and did not feel comfortable moving to live with me in Detroit. We liked each other a lot. But the personal trust just wasn't there.

As that second visit to Chicago went on, tensions and insecurities that we had experienced in college began to return. I talked about traveling to Europe. Karen asked, "Are you considering going there in the near future?"

I said "I might."

That evening, after a fairly intense day, I offered a plan for the next morning—I can't remember the specifics.

Karen responded, "I don't want to do that." Then she paused added, "I can get you to do things that I want, but you won't be able to get me to do things you want."

I asked, "Why is that?"

Karen responded, "Because you're in love with me and I'm not in love with you."

We were both silent for a couple of minutes. Then Karen said, "That was pretty heavy. Wasn't it?"

I nodded my assent.

*****

The next morning, I hitchhiked back to Detroit. On the way, I thought a lot about what had transpired. I wasn't angry. I was hurt. But I also realized that for me, peace of mind was more important than falling in love. I did not want to duplicate my parents' marriage. I didn't want the sadness or anger they experienced. I realized that part of my quest was trying to find out what a good partnership between a man and a woman can be—what it should be.

I wasn't there yet. But I was learning. My friendship with Russ included qualities that I felt would be a part of a successful relationship with a woman—things like respect, trust—and give and take. I decided that maybe I needed to try to build a friendship with a woman that grew into love, rather than fall in love with somebody—and then try to turn it into a friendship.

*****

Upon my return to Detroit, I went back to my routine. But for the first time since I'd come to Detroit, I felt empty. While work continued to be interesting, it lacked meaning.

I realized that it was time to move on. I considered the various places that I might want to go. My father had once said he had acquaintances in Paris, France who might be able to help me get a work permit and find a job. I called my dad and learned he could give me a letter of introduction, but no guarantees.

That was good enough.

So, a couple of days after I returned from Chicago, I told Russ, "I think I am going to pull another Roger. It's time for me to move on. I'm going to visit my dad in New York. Then I think I'll move to Paris."

Russ knew me pretty well and was not surprised by my decision. He applauded my plan to move to Paris and wished me luck in finding a path that offered the meaning for which I was looking.

*****

As I look back on Detroit, it seems like the city's loss of prosperity had resulted in an environment that allowed colorful people to step forward. Living there exposed Russ and me to people who were special. Whether it was my co-workers at the hospital; a local theater with a Groucho Marx Night offering prizes for the best Marx Brothers costume; a food co-op with a sweet young woman who seemed like a flower child from Haight Ashbury, circa 1967; or a young high school dropout who dressed as if she was in the seventeenth century—my life was constantly enriched by the people of Detroit.

*****

It was the March of 1973. I had worked at Grace Hospital for four and a half months. It had been a deeply amazing experience. But I was ready to move on. I gave notice to the hospital, bid farewell to Russ and to my workmates. Then I hitchhiked out of Detroit, heading east.

12—Life in Paris

I had saved enough of my Detroit earnings to purchase a roundtrip ticket to Europe and have five hundred dollars remaining to begin a life in France. If I wasn't able to find a job in Paris, I would travel across Europe until my funds were exhausted; then return to the United States.

The night before my flight to Europe, my hands were shaking so badly that it was difficult to fold my clothing as I packed my backpack. The uncertainty of what was ahead was scary.

*****

Early, the next morning, my father drove me to Kennedy Airport where I caught an Icelandic Airline flight to Luxembourg. From there, I would take a train into Paris.

On the flight over, I sat next to two American college students heading to Europe for a month of fun. Their light-hearted attitude was a welcome distraction. While the stewardesses poured drinks for passengers, one of my seatmates removed a full bottle of wine from below the drink cart. By the time we'd finished that bottle, we were drunk enough to sleep for the rest of the flight.

We landed in Luxemburg in the morning. My seatmates were also heading for Paris. I traveled with them to the Luxemburg train station where we caught a train to Paris. In Paris, we took the Metro to the Latin Quarter, found an affordable hotel room, ate a late-night pizza dinner and crashed for the night.

*****

The next morning, I said goodbye to my travel companions. Once more, I was beginning a new life in a new city. However, in addition to exploring another city, I needed to speak another language.

In college, I had been required to complete four terms of a foreign language. My ability to learn French was less than stellar. The C- grade I received in French I was the highest grade I received in the series. In French II, I got a D. I failed French III the first time I took it—then got a D- in my second attempt. My French IV professor later admitted he gave me a passing grade just to get me out of the French department. But in Paris, in spite of those mediocre college results, I found I could successfully communicate in French.

*****

My father had given me a letter of introduction to an acquaintance in Paris named Jack Egle (pronounced *eagle*). He said Mr. Egle might be able to help me land a position in Paris. A couple of days after arriving in the City of Light, I called Jack Egle and introduced myself, telling him I was looking for employment. Egle offered to meet me at his office.

The following day, I met Jack Egle at his non-profit organization, the Council on International Educational Exchange. It was located on rue Pierre Charron, next door to the headquarters of Paris Match Magazine and only two blocks away from the Champs-Élysées, the main artery of business and culture in Paris.

The Council on International Educational Exchange sold discount airline tickets to students who were traveling to major cities throughout Europe. As I entered its first-floor customer service area, I saw students from all over the world speaking a broad array of languages. A few minutes after I informed an employee I was there to meet with Mr. Egle, I was approached by a strikingly attractive young woman with a lyrical Irish accent. She introduced herself to me as Bernadette.

Bernadette led me upstairs. A few minutes later, I was sitting in a large leather chair in Jack Egle's office. Egle, a short, nicely groomed, middle-aged business man entered the office and shook my hand. He told me to call him Jack and asked me to tell him about myself.

I was brief, telling Jack I'd grown up in the Midwest, graduated from college and was taking a few years off to see the world. I explained I wanted a job that would cover my living expenses in Paris.

Jack Egle told me he understood my situation. The Council was formed right after the war to help American students travel to Europe and he arrived in Paris shortly after that—on an adventure a little like mine. He found a job working at the Council in 1946 and became head of its Paris Office in 1951.

*****

The Council's busy season was about to start. There were a couple of job openings that might interest me. They worked Mondays through Fridays plus Saturday mornings. One of the jobs was a six-month position coordinating student group arrivals and departures. It paid thirteen hundred francs or three hundred twenty-five dollars a month.

The other position was ongoing. It paid fifteen hundred francs a month plus benefits. It supported the backbone of the Council's operations, a computer system located in Copenhagen that tracked reservations for multiple airlines throughout Europe. The person in the position would type reservation and other flight data onto a tickertape, then send the tickertape through a telex machine—a sort of telegraph data input machine—to the computer system in Copenhagen.

The interview lasted only fifteen minutes. I told Egle I was interested in the telexist position. He called out to the young woman who had brought me upstairs. "Bernadette—Roger is our new telexist. He'll start tomorrow. Would you please take him around, introduce him to other Council employees and show him his office?"

*****

Bernadette was neatly dressed with long carefully groomed with long auburn hair. I was in awe of her voluptuous body, upbeat Irish accent and gracious demeanor. She guided me through the building introducing me to a dozen employees—from England, Ireland, the Netherlands, Czechoslovakia, the United States and, of course, France. The last person I met was Roger Darmon (pronounced ro-jay' darmo'), a Frenchman who was in charge of Council day-to-day operations.

Then Bernadette handed me off to Paula, Roger Darmon's courteous and efficient secretary. Paula (pronounced *pow'-la*) was Dutch. She took me to into a large work room that would be my office. It had windows across one wall and was furnished with three telex machines (they looked like heavy duty electric typewriters), two tables, a large leather desk chair, several file cabinets and a miniature ping-pong table.

Paula described the work I would do. Several Council staff would bring me memos and reports to type into telex machines. The telex machines' output was ticker tape that I would feed into little gizmos that instantaneously transmitted the information to the computer in Denmark or to the Council's New York office.

Paula warmly congratulated me on being hired and told me she would train me to use the machines the following day.

I was elated. Doors had opened for me once again! I was about to live in Paris and absorb the French culture while living the fascinating life of an expatriate! The ghosts of F. Scott Fitzgerald and Ernest Hemingway should be put on notice! My version of Walter Mitty, the young, adventurous writer, had come to live in Paris!

*****

That evening, after I returned to the youth hostel, I was given a roommate from Great Britain. Peter had just received his bachelor of arts degree from Cambridge University. He had a stuffy attitude, carefully combed (but slightly out of control) thick reddish hair and a bushy red mustache. In the tan and brown wool tweed suit he always wore, Peter looked and acted like a cartoon lampooning British aristocracy.

That evening, Peter and I went for out for a glass of wine on Boulevard Saint Michel. We passed a couple of attractive young British women. I recognized the opportunity and tried to seize it, starting a conversation with them. I achieved no success and Peter offered no help. So, in order to impress these women, I pulled out my trump card. "My friend here," I said confidently, "recently graduated from Cambridge."

One of the women turned to the other and said sarcastically, "Oh—then I guess we're among privileged company".

Peter quietly muttered something about the two young women's' lack of class as they briskly walked way.

Afterwards, Peter explained to me that these were lower-class women. We should not be interested in them. I could only shake my head—what was he thinking? They were good looking! What an arrogant dufus!

That was my first lesson in social class distinctions as practiced in Great Britain.

*****

The following morning, I took the Metro—Paris' wonderful underground rapid transit system—into work. I was ready to start work at nine.

As Paula poured me a cup of coffee, she informed me that American coffee companies bought the best coffee beans in the world and ruined them by doing a lousy job of roasting and grinding the beans. "Americans add insult to injury," she concluded, "by destroying any remaining quality in the beans by overcooking the coffee in their aluminum percolators."

I drank the coffee. It was excellent. I had worked at the Council for only an hour and had already learned something!

*****

Throughout that first day of work, Council employees stopped by my office to chat. Some had been introduced to me the previous day. I was meeting others for the first time. Without exception though, all of the people who I met were bright, positive and ready to have a good time. Most had a college education. Many had come to Paris because they wanted to enrich their lives with the magic of the City of Light. And while all of them needed a job to fund their adventures, they saw no reason not to have fun while making their living. It was clear to me that the Council was going to be an enjoyable place to work.

Paula taught me how to do my job. My most important responsibility was carried out at the end of each work day. I had to type flight information representing all new flights available for booking, all new reservations and all cancellations. My telex machine input had to be perfect. Any format errors or typos would cause the Copenhagen computer to reject my entire submission. Each evening, I was not be able to leave work until I received confirmation from Copenhagen that my data transmission had been successfully transmitted.

The rigorous perfection computers require was totally new to me. I quickly was forced to learn that slow and deliberate beats fast and efficient. And fortunately, my typing skills were pretty good.

*****

My workdays followed a consistent pattern. Each morning, prior to arriving at work at nine, I picked up a single breakfast pastry from a nearby patisserie. It was difficult choosing between the lemon tarts, napoleons, apple tarts, eclairs and croissants—they were all so wonderful. I carried that pastry into work. There I ate it and washed it down with Paula's excellent coffee.

Morning telex workload was driven by other employees' production. In the afternoon around one, I took my lunch hour. After lunch, I focused on telexes being sent to and received from New York. At the end of the day, my attention turned to the input and transmission of the day's flight reservations. I generally left the office by six or six-thirty. But if a time sensitive document was handed to me just before I planned on leaving the office, I stayed until it was complete.

*****

While there was a wide array of excellent restaurants and charcuteries near my office, I couldn't afford to go out to lunch often. I usually purchased my lunch—a baguette, some cheese and a piece of fruit on my way to work washing that down with a glass of wine from an open bottle of wine I kept in my office. After lunch, I read a book or walked, exploring nearby neighborhoods, gazing at elegant merchandise displays in store windows or appreciating an area's architecture.

The office celebrated many employees' birthdays by going out for lunch as a group. Those meals were fun—the wine kept flowing. These celebratory lunches often did not break up until after three in the afternoon and sometimes continued in the office (playing ping-pong in my office). Those festivities were not the only time we played ping-pong. We played during lunch on rainy days. On a couple of slow days, the games went well into the afternoon. Ping-pong on such a small table involves a lot of spin on the ball, some soft shots and a few slams.

*****

In a letter, my father spoke highly about a small café that was about a mile from the youth hostel. He told me the couple who ran it were warm and gracious, the food excellent and the cost reasonable. On the first Saturday afternoon after I started at the Council, I walked over to the café. It was located on a quiet residential street named rue Poliveau.

I introduced myself to the restaurant's owners, Madame Gaby and Monsieur Émile. They invited me into the café's dining room. It was simply furnished with four or five wooden tables covered with red and white checkered tablecloths. Table were surrounded by wooden ladder-back chairs. The small dining room's walls displayed a series of framed black and white photographs. Near the café's entrance was an old wooden bar with a few bottles of liquor lined up on a shelf behind it.

Monsieur Émile and Madame Gaby were both about sixty years old. He was medium height, a little over-weight and always seemed to be smoking a cigarette. He had a mustache, carefully combed hair and dressed simply in dark pants and short-sleeved white shirts. She was petite, had dark medium-length hair and dressed in a simple cotton print dress with an apron. They seemed like a couple one might expect to have met in a small French village in the early 1950s. Their gentle manner was unlike the more aloof demeanor I had observed in so many Parisians.

Their cafe was a part of their rooming house and they only served dinners to those patrons who rented a room from them or lived on rue Poliveau. They turned others interested diners away.

Madame Gaby and Monsieur Émile's fond memories of my father was the basis of their offer for me to eat my dinners at their restaurant. The cost for each meal was reasonable—six francs—the equivalent of a dollar and a half. I told them I was interested and explained that I was looking for a room—something that was less expensive than the youth hostel. Did they have any rooms available?

No, they didn't. But Monsieur Émile informed me that the Hotel de la Renaissance, across the street, might have a room.

*****

I left the café, crossed rue Poliveau and walked another thirty feet to the Hotel de la Renaissance. It was a four-story stucco building with a large front door on which the paint was peeling from decades of wear. I knocked. No one answered. I opened the heavy door, walking into a large open entrance and calling out, "Est-ce que quelqu'un est à la maison?"

After a couple of minutes, a short, plump woman came down a broad wooden stairway. She was probably about seventy years old and was wearing an old housecoat with a flowered print head scarf. Our conversation in French began with her asking if she could help me.

"I am living and working in Paris. Monsieur Émile suggested I inquire if your hotel has any vacancies."

She responded with motherly warmth. "Yes, I have a room for rent. I am Madame Olga. Please follow me. I will show you to your room."

Madame Olga led me up the solid but creaky stairs to the second floor. She removed a large ring of old skeleton keys from her apron pocket, selected one and slid it into the lock on a door that had to be over a couple of hundred years old. She carefully turned the key, then opened the door to reveal a large room from another era.

The room was about twenty by fourteen feet. It had a ten-foot-high ceiling and was furnished with an iron frame double bed, a large ancient wooden wardrobe, a simple wooden chair and a small wooden table. There was also a sink with only one faucet—the building did not have heated water. The room was lit by a single light bulb dangling from the ceiling in the center of the room. The well-worn unfinished wood floor and the room's wallpaper that featured large flowers spoke to me from the last century. On the rue Poliveau-side of the room were eight-foot-tall, lace curtain-covered, glass-paned double doors that opened onto a shallow balcony.

Madame Olga showed me the commode on the street level—a Turkish toilet. If you have never seen or used a Turkish toilet, you need not feel cheated. It is a six-inch hole in the center of a shower stall sized room. Hotel de la Renaissance had no bath or shower.

Madame Olga informed me that the rent for the room was three hundred francs per month—the equivalent of seventy-five dollars. That was much less than I was paying at the youth hostel. I told her I would move in the next morning and thanked her. Then I walked across the street and confirmed with Madame Gaby and Monsieur Émile that I would eat my dinners, Monday through Friday, in their restaurant.

Hotel de la Renaissance was a dream come true. Sunday morning, I checked out of the youth hostel, carried my belongings to my new room at the hotel and paid my first month's rent to Madame Olga.

*****

The following Monday evening at 7 o'clock, I walked across the street from Hotel de la Renaissance to enjoy the first of many wonderful dinners at Madame Gaby and Monsieur Émile's restaurant. The half dozen patrons who dined at the cafe were all men, ranging in age from thirty to seventy. They were all originally from French provinces. They lacked the typical Parisian snobbery and each patron welcomed me with jovial warmth.

The dinner routine I observed that evening was be repeated each time I ate there. Before dinner, two or three patrons arrived early. We would stand at the small bar and order drinks from Monsieur Émile. We each drank pastis, an anise flavored yellow liquor. When mixed with ice cold water, pastis turns a milky white. It is a very refreshing aperitif. Each patron had their favorite brand of pastis which they drank without exception. Those brands included *Pernod, Ricard, Gervais* and *Pastis 51*.

Typically, one of the patrons would say, "*Monsieur Émile, un boisson pour mes amis.*" (A drink for my friends). Then Monsieur Émile would serve each of us a glass of our preferred brand of pastis. My brand was *Ricard*. I liked the sharp edge of its flavor as compared to what seemed to me like a less distinct flavor of the other brands.

If there were two of us at the bar, we would each drink two glasses of our favorite pastis. If there were four of us, we would each down four. After each patron had purchased a round of pastis, smoked a cigarette, toasted the company of their friends and enjoyed their aperitifs, Madame Gaby would announce that it was time to sit down at the dinner table and eat, "*On mange maintenant.*"

*****

Madame Gaby and Monsieur Émile sat at their own table. The patrons, which now included me, sat at a second table. Each evening's menu had several courses—small simple tasty servings with as many slices of baguette as we wanted plus a small carafe of red wine. The first course was either a salad or a soup. After that, Madame Gaby brought each of us our main plate that included a small amount of meat, some sort of potato or rice and a serving of vegetables. Finally, for desert Madame Gaby would ask each of us if we preferred fruit or cheese. "*Monsieur Roger, fromage ou fruit?*"

From the moment I entered the restaurant for pastis before dinner until I left the restaurant after my cheese or fruit, we enjoyed one another, shared stories and laughed. I was the only person in the restaurant, or for that matter on all of rue Poliveau, who spoke English. So, I was forced to either improve my French or embarrass myself trying. While I had not done well in French in college, *on apprend á parler Francais vitement quand on bois du vin Francais rapidément.* (One learns to speak French quickly when one drinks French wine rapidly).

It was a joy to break bread each evening with these kind and gentle French country folk who treated each other with such warmth and respect. I never heard a harsh word from any of them during those meals. And laughter— laughter was a constant element in all discourse.

*****

Hotel de la Renaissance met every expectation I could possibly have had for a home in Paris. The accommodations were simple, but the room's aura was grand—straight out of the 19th century. At night, I slept with my balcony glass doors wide open. I awoke in the morning to fresh air and the sound of rue Poliveau being hosed down by street cleaners. The hotel's major missing feature—no shower or bathing facility—was addressed easily. In order to take a shower, I simply walked down the street and paid two francs to use the public shower.

After a month living at 42 rue Poliveau, I bought a used classical guitar for fifty dollars. I hadn't played guitar for over a year and was thrilled to find an affordable instrument with such a soft tone. With it, I purchased a wonderful classical guitar book, *Méthode de Guitare*, by Ferdinando Carulli. The book, written in 1810, had compositions reminiscent of baroque chamber music. They were not too difficult to play and I enjoyed their lyrical runs and soft harmonies.

Practicing the guitar gave me peace. At one point, I fantasized about leaving my job with the Council and playing classical guitar in Paris' metro stations. I figured that would be an excellent way to learn guitar well while earning a living. I demonstrated common sense by choosing to ignore that bohemian fantasy. My guitar skills were not that great.

Each evening after I finished work and return to my room, I would practice guitar for half an hour. Playing guitar after work turned the intensity of the work day into the peace of a beautiful evening. After practicing, I would cross the street, drink my pastis, dine and converse with my friends.

*****

In order to open a personal bank account, a significant deposit was required. Since few of my co-workers were in a position to meet that standard, the Council had negotiated an agreement with a nearby bank to cash Council employee paychecks. Twice a month during my lunch hour, I went to the bank and cashed my check. That evening, I paid half my monthly rent my accumulated restaurant tab.

I carefully managed my expenditures. When I spent too much early in a pay period, I would be penniless at its end. When that happened, I'd walk to work and skip some weekend meals.

*****

Paris was full of interesting people and I was always open to getting to know someone new through a chance encounter. That approach worked well because many other young Parisians approached life with a similar laissez-faire attitude. As a result, I made more friends in Paris than in any other city in which I'd lived. Still, there were times when I was lonely.

The Cinematheque is Paris' museum of film. It is located across the Seine from the Eiffel Tower and has one of the largest international film archives in the world. Every two hours, the Cinematheque showed a different film. No film was shown more than once in a year and admission tickets were affordable.

I never saw a schedule of Cinematheque films. When I chose to go, I knew whatever film was showing would be a wonderful. It might be modern or maybe sixty years old. It could be Latin-American or Russian or Japanese or Italian or French or American. It made no difference to me. I knew it would be a classic. I would get in the ticket line; buy ticket; and never be disappointed.

One evening, while I stood in line waiting to see a film, I asked the woman ahead of me in my mediocre French, "Excuse me Madame, but what film is playing this evening?"

She responded to me (also in French), "Oh, the film playing this evening is the *Lake of the Blue Clouds* by Mikio Naruse. It is a wonderful Japanese film from the early 1950s and has not been shown in Paris for almost twenty years. If you are attending this film without knowing it would be shown, you are most fortunate."

The woman was petite. She had dark hair and dark eyes and was about forty. Her husband who was standing next to her was about the same age and height as his wife. He also had dark eyes and dark hair. His graying beard was carefully trimmed. They were both dressed in a simple, casual manner.

We chatted in French for a minute or two. Suddenly, with an accent that sounded like a Jew from the Bronx, she began to speak English. "But you are an American and I should speak to you in English."

Our conversation continued in English until we entered the theater. After the film, we continued to speak. Her name was Madeleine Gorovitz. Her husband's name was Matheus. She was Jewish and had been raised in Paris. When the Nazis had taken Paris, her parents were arrested. Throughout the rest of Germany's occupation, she and her sister were hidden in a Paris convent by nuns. Matheus was a Brazilian architect. His grandfather had been known as *the great rabbi of Rio de Janeiro*. Matheus and Madeleine had two small children, Sabine and Justine. The family lived in Paris rather than Brazil due to a difficult job market in Brazil. Their hope was to someday return to Brazil.

That evening, as we said good night, we exchanged addresses and they invited me to dinner for the following Saturday. It was my first invitation to someone's home since I had arrived in Paris. I was so pleased.

*****

Saturday evening as I walked to their home, I purchased a good bottle of Sauterne at a small wine shop on rue Poliveau.

Matheus and Madeleine's home was on a narrow, cobble-stoned, block-long street named rue Villa Seurat. I realized it was named in honor of the French post-impressionist Georges Seurat, but did not learn until years later that Seurat had actually lived at that location in a home long since gone. The buildings I saw on rue Villa Seurat had been built and designed in the 1920s—long after Seurat was gone. But with rue Villa Seurat, Paris had created a center for artists' studios. In the 1930s, Henry Miller and Anaïs Nin wrote some of their most famous books while living on that short street. Miller wrote *Tropic of Cancer* and Nin wrote *House of Incest*. Other celebrated artists also lived there over the years including the surrealist Salvador Dali and Andre' Derain, who along with Henri Matisse, created a new style of painting called Fauvism.

Henry Miller described rue Villa Seurat accurately. "The whole street is given up to quiet joyous work. Every house contains a writer, painter, musician, sculptor or actor."

I could tell rue Villa Seurat was still home to artists because, as I walked to the Gorovitz's door, I could hear violins practicing scales.

*****

Matheus and Madeleine greeted me warmly. Madeleine expressed pleasure over the bottle of wine. "Look Matheus, Roger has brought us a bottle of Sauterne! I don't know how long it has been since we've had a wonderful bottle of Sauterne."

I later learned that Sauterne is a dessert wine. Even though I had brought it to accompany the meal. Madeleine had been kind enough to ignore my faux pas.

Their two-story studio apartment was dramatically designed. Its high-ceilinged main living area had a sixteen-by-sixteen-foot window-wall that looked out on a green space. Across from the window-wall was the apartment's entrance, a small kitchen, a bathroom and the kids' sleeping space. Over those rooms was a loft in which Madeleine and Matheus slept. Matheus and Madeleine told me that the apartment once had been the home of a famous Israeli architect. An Israeli film crew once asked to film its interior.

For dinner, we had a baguette with butter, sliced onions, Gouda cheese, leek soup made from a Knorr dry soup mix and the bottle of Sauterne. The simplicity of the meal was driven by their tight budget. But the pure joy of dining with them made the dinner taste like an elegant feast.

*****

I saw Matheus and Madeleine often. Through them, I met Daniel and Armelle, their close bohemian, socialist friends. Daniel was Chinese-American. He had grown up in San Francisco and always wore blue jeans and a button-down shirt. Daniel (pronounced don-ee-elle') was loud and sarcastic. His wife Armelle was a French aristocrat, disgusted with modern materialism. Her politics and nonconformist lifestyle had alienated her from her upper-class family. Armelle was beautiful. She had long wavy dark blond hair and was always beautifully dressed—often in long dark skirts accompanied by delicate lace-trimmed white blouses.

The day I met Armelle and Daniel, I had gone to a local café to drink wine and play pinball with Matheus and Madeleine. While the men were busy taking turns showing that we were really pinball wizards, Madeleine and Armelle sat at a table drinking *petite blancs*, small glasses of white wine.

I had been reading F. Scott Fitzgerald's *Tender is the Night*. It was sitting on the cafe table. Armelle picked the book up and opened it. In English, with a sensuous French accent, Armelle said, "Oh how wonderful, I love Fitzgerald's writing. You know the most wonderful thing about an F. Scott Fitzgerald book? If you open—any of his books—to any page—to any paragraph, the sentence you read will be a

182

complete image communicated in a perfectly written sentence. Let me show you."

Armelle opened *Tender is the Night* and randomly selected and read sentences aloud. Each sentence and the image it portrayed was clear and complete. Armelle was right!

That interlude was fascinating in many regards. First of all, I gained a better appreciation for the skill of F. Scott Fitzgerald. But I was even more impressed by this beautiful woman who had been raised speaking French, yet had developed such a sophisticated appreciation of literature from another language.

*****

Matheus and Madeleine's children were completely charming. Sabine was five. Her brother Justine was three. One evening, I volunteered to babysit them. The highlight of the evening occurred when Sabine came out of the kids' space dressed in one of her mother's old silk dresses adorned with a variety of costume jewelry including a rhinestone tiara. As she walked toward me in a dress that was much too large, Sabine proclaimed, "*Je suis la reine. Je suis la reine.*" (I am the queen. I am the queen.)

Moments later Justine came out dressed in a similar outfit saying, with the babyish enunciation of a three-year-old, "*Je suis la reine aussi. Je suis la reine aussi.*" (I am the queen also. I am the queen also.)

*****

I had several wonderful get-togethers with Matheus, Madeleine, Daniel and Armelle. Unfortunately, about a month after I met her, Madeleine announced that Matheus had been offered a position as professor of architecture at the University of Brasilia. They would leave Paris for Brazil in a few weeks. I was so disappointed. They were the best friends I'd made since I'd graduated. Now, they were going away.

Madeleine told me that their apartment rent was paid one month in advance and their landlord was unwilling to return that month's rent to them. She said I could have their apartment, at no cost, for that month. And so, when the Gorovitz family departed for Brazil, I moved into their rue Villa Seurat apartment. The month I lived there was wonderful. But a month passes quickly and I soon needed a plan for where I would live.

*****

I'd met a young Argentinean couple. Maria was a college student and Juan was an unemployed film-maker. Maria was tall, well-tanned, had long light brown hair and had an almost muscular beauty. Maria had been raised within Argentina's privileged class and was a very gentle person. Juan had dark hair and a short-trimmed beard. He had grown up in the poverty of Rio de Janeiro and had a confident, controlling demeanor. They both dressed in Latin American white cotton peasant-style shirts and pants.

Being with Juan and Maria was always interesting. Juan brought an adventurous *on-the-edge* attitude to everything he did. One fun evening, he drove erratically down the Champs-Elysées and then raced in circles around the Arc de Triomphe. Maria laughed while I used their 8mm movie camera to film the monument, the pedestrians and other drivers.

They once invited me to join them at a friend's get-together. I was the only person at the party who was not from Latin America. The apartment was decorated with posters of Che Guevara and other radicals celebrating the ongoing revolution. I told the apartment's Puerto Rican host how much I liked his place.

He responded, "The things that made this apartment special are thanks to the generosity of my friends."

I said, "I wish there was something I could give you that would make your apartment more special."

He replied, "You can. There is. Give us your head."

Clearly, he did not have warm feelings toward a young, white, privileged American.

*****

When Juan heard I needed to leave my apartment on rue Villa Seurat, he suggested the three of us get an apartment together. Maria was about to complete her degree at a private college in Paris and had to move out of her college housing. They had planned to get a place together. But if I joined them, they could get a larger apartment.

I was game.

A few days later, I contacted Juan and Maria to remind them that I had to move out of my place in a few days. Juan told me they had not yet found an apartment, but I could stay with Maria until they found one. That seemed fine. I visited Maria and found she was living in a women's college dormitory. Her small room had one twin bed. Maria attracted me. But I wasn't sure about all of the dynamics attached to that situation. I decided I better find some other place to live.

I stopped by to check with Madame Olga at the Hotel de la Renaissance. She had a vacancy and welcomed me back. Madame Gaby and Monsieur Émile were also pleased to have me rejoin the patrons at their restaurant. So, with a huge sigh of relief, I refreshed my appreciation of the Hotel de la Renaissance, the cordial dinners at Chez Gaby and Émile and the gentle folk of rue Poliveau.

13—Learning about Style

My father spent much of his life trying to understand humanity in the face of the viciousness he had experienced as a young man. Such a focus on mankind's cruelty is not unexpected given that he escaped from Nazi Germany as a seventeen-year-old Jew and lost his mother and other loved ones in the holocaust. He taught me to try to understand life rather than just react to it. Partly because of this, I became fairly cerebral—existing in a world of ideas.

In Paris, I forced a change in that approach. I pushed myself to see, hear, touch, taste and smell what was around me. I was constantly drawn into the freshness of unique moments—walking in a park, sitting in a café or watching children sail toy boats in a pond. I made myself notice details—and appreciate them. In so doing, I discovered a richness in life that was new for me.

*****

I enjoyed Paris' museums without haste, one art piece at a time, rather than by quickly moving through a museum, trying to see as many artworks as possible. I particularly liked smaller museums that focused on one artist.

The Rodin Museum was my favorite small museum. Located in what was once Rodin's home, studio and garden, it offered many of Rodin's best-known statues. I loved walking through his 19th century home which displayed fine paintings by his impressionist friends, period furniture, sculpture studies and worn parquet wooden floors. I would wander through its park-like grounds which included *Monument to Balzac, Gates of Hell* and *The Kiss.* Sometimes I would spend a lunch hour walking along garden paths or sitting on a bench in front of one of those magnificent statues, meditating on Rodin's grand vision of humankind.

Afterwards, I returned to the Council reinvigorated.

*****

I had always gotten a cheap haircut when my hair badly needed it—probably more accurately stated, five weeks after it was badly needed. When I moved to Paris, my hair was shoulder length. I quickly noted that that was not in vogue in France. My long hair shouted that I was an American. When I finally decided to get a haircut, I learned that Paris does not have cheap barbershops. The French go to a *coiffure* who first gives the customer a shampoo; then skillfully cuts and styles their hair.

I went to a *coiffure* and liked it. I'd never had another person shampoo my hair. It felt wonderful. I relished the experience as well as the outcome, leaving the coiffure with a nice haircut and a fresh state of mind. During my stay in Paris, my hair kept getting shorter and shorter—I so enjoyed getting my hair cut.

*****

Clothing was expensive in Paris. My co-workers, even though they certainly spent more for each garment, had fewer pieces of clothing than most people I had known. A French woman might have two quality outfits with interchangeable components. This allowed her to dress differently on different days for less cost than a mediocre, but much more extensive, wardrobe.

The quality of French fabric and the styling and tailoring of their garments was always superb. But each article was expensive. Unfortunately, on my income, I couldn't afford to be too fashionable. But, in watching how

Parisians dressed, I learned a lesson of life. Quality is more important than quantity.

Another similar lesson related to the size of servings in French restaurants. Servings were smaller than those I was used to in the States. However, each food item was finely prepared and nicely presented. A meal became satisfying because of the quality of its ingredients, preparation and presentation; not because of the portion's size.

This principle of quality trumping quantity is fundamental to the French culture.

*****

When traveling to work, a friend's apartment, or a museum, I would often forego the Metro, instead taking a route which would pass through streets and neighborhoods I hadn't seen. The time investment of leaving a little earlier was paid back with new opportunities to appreciate Paris. My walks took me past parks where I watched children play and families meander. I looked at storefronts with fascinating displays and was introduced to buildings that echoed the fantastic history of Paris. Those promenades were oftentimes more memorable than whatever awaited me at my destination.

*****

My room on rue Poliveau was near the *Jardin des Plantes*, the main botanical garden in Paris. The park was over 350 years old. Its gardens were a combination of beautifully arranged plants and trees, old greenhouses that seemed like sculptural monuments, a museum, a zoo and countless families out for a stroll. I used to enjoy walking through the park; often stopping to watch a group of old men play chess at tables in a corner of the park. I was fascinated with those chess players and their unique styles of play.

One beautiful Sunday afternoon, I was standing next to seven or eight other onlookers, watching a chess game conclude. The winner, a heavy man—probably about seventy, dressed in a worn, buttoned up, royal blue wool suit and red beret—had already won four games in a row against an assortment of characters. He looked up at me, and said in French, "You. You are next."

The other onlookers turned their attention to me and waited for me to sit down at the chess table. I had no sooner taken a seat than he made his first move. I was ready for a fast game, having seen how quickly other games had been played, but this first move was really fast. I played it safe with a quick response to his opening move. However, it took him less than a second to follow up with his second move. I responded in kind. He continued to play at that pace and my responses remained quick and conservative.

This game was moving even more rapidly than other games I'd seen him play. But I didn't know what else to do but move quickly and stay cautious.

As I considered one of my moves, I touched one of my bishops. My opponent said, "*Touché.*" I had touched a piece. He was telling me I had to move the bishop I had touched. That was a new rule for me. But if that's how the game was being played, then that was how I had to play it. I moved my bishop.

Playing chess at that pace—especially when you are not feeling confident enough to communicate in your opponent's language and a half-dozen of people are watching—it's an intense experience. Having a new rule thrown into the mix made it that much tougher. Amazingly,

I didn't make a mistake and the game continued to a point where we each had five or six pieces left on the board.

We'd made a sufficient number moves without either party losing a piece that the game should have been called a draw. But I didn't know the French word for *draw*. The small audience watching us seemed to understand my dilemma and was amused.

About ten moves after a draw should have been called, I lost the game. By then, it was a relief. I was happy to give up my seat at the chess table.

*****

I read constantly. One especially relevant book was Ernest Hemingway's *A Movable Feast*. In it, Hemingway talks about the people he met in Paris and the unique qualities of the city. In the preface of his book, Hemingway makes a statement that rang true for me. "If you are lucky enough to have lived in Paris as a young man, then where ever you go for the rest of your life, it stays with you, for Paris is a movable feast."

Both *A Moveable Feast* and George Orwell's book *Down and Out in Paris and London* confirmed that I was not the first young person to come to Paris to try to discover richness in life. And I knew that I would not be the last. Almost every day, I met someone on a sharp personal learning curve who had moved to Paris because they were excited about life and were ready to become a larger person.

Since the end of World War I, countless young American and British expatriates living in Paris had bought English language books at the Shakespeare and Company bookstore. I enjoyed the shop's ambience. Many great authors had perused its bookshelves. It was almost like I could sense their spirits.

I found purchasing a book there to be a wonderful task for a weekend afternoon. After buying a book, I would take it to a park and read. Spending a day like that was satisfying.

*****

Work, of course, consumed the biggest part of my week. As the summer passed, I developed skill on the telex machine, improved my French and became better acquainted with my co-workers.

My confidence in how well I did my job helped me feel comfortable enough to have fun at work in new ways. In 1958, China's Chairman Mao Tse-tung initiated a grand economic and cultural plan called *The Great Leap Forward*. It was short-lived. Mao ended the program in 1960. But *The Great Leap Forward* has always seemed to me to be the sort of inane political campaign that an over-the-edge leader like Mussolini might have initiated.

In mid-summer, I began to create tongue-in-cheek political posters to celebrate my own version of *The Great Leap Forward*. Each day, on the door of my office, I posted a single page hand-written statement that mimicked Mao's revolutionary program.

Examples of daily posters included:

"Part of the Great Leap Forward is to drink an extra bottle of wine at lunch in order to stimulate the economy—and the body."

"Part of the Great Leap Forward is for all future telex requests to be submitted in triplicate. This will triple Council productivity."

Laughter in the workplace is a good thing and I was having fun doing my job.

*****

Roger Darmon, our chief operating officer at times stumbled with English grammar. One day, I typed and telexed a memo from Mr. Darmon to the lead operations manager in our New York office. As I typed the memo, I noticed several grammatical errors and corrected them.

The next morning, Roger asked me if I had made any grammatical improvements to his memo. I responded that I had. He thanked me and told me he had noticed and I had done a good job.

That praise felt really good.

The following day, Roger had me send a memo to a business partner. The memo included a fair amount of technical information. I again made small improvements to the memo. When I was done, I was pleased with my product and sent it on its way.

The following morning, Roger again asked me if I had made improvements to his memo. I proudly affirmed that I had. Roger explained that unfortunately, as I improved his memo, I had also changed its meaning significantly. He asked me not to make changes in the future.

I felt quite deflated.

*****

One morning, when I entered my office, something had changed. My large leather chair was gone. It was a comfortable chair and its castors allowed me to roll between telex machines. In its place was a simple desk chair. I asked Paula and Bernadette if they had any idea who had taken my chair. They didn't. I asked others. A co-worker told me she had seen the Council's Vice President for Finance checking out my chair the previous day. I went to his office which was on another floor.

When I got there, he was meeting with someone I didn't know. But I saw he was sitting on my chair. I excused myself as I walked into his office. Once I had his attention (and the attention of whomever he was meeting with), I asked him if he knew what had happened to my chair. He explained to me that he had needed a better chair, so he had taken mine. But he authorized me to purchase any chair I wanted from his assistant's furniture catalogue.

I responded, "I don't want another chair. I want my chair."

He self-righteously stood up and, in order to embarrass me in front of his business associate, said in a loud angry voice, "Here! If you want this chair, take it now!"

I said, "Thank you" and rolled my chair out of his office, into the elevator and back to my office.

That story has always amazed me because it describes so well my fearless lack of judgment.

But I had my chair.

*****

Each year, the Council hired a half dozen young Americans to supplement staff during the summer months. Many of those temporary employees hung out together. By doing this, I realized they were insulating themselves from the French people as well as other international residents of Paris. That was the last thing I wanted to do. Living in Paris was an opportunity to meet and get to know new and interesting people.

I chose not to socialize with my co-workers outside of work.

*****

The International Communist Festival brought together progressives and radicals from across all of France in an intellectual and cultural phenomenon. An American expatriate I had met invited me, his French girlfriend and a young French woman to attend the festival with him. I was enthusiastic about attending the event and especially pleased to have a date. The festival was held in a large park in a northeastern suburb of Paris. At the fair, I saw hundreds of interesting booths and each booth presented some aspect of leftist politics. One booth was operated by Angela Davis, the highly visible American black power activist.

The entertainment highlight of the festival was a rock concert featuring Jerry Lee Lewis and Chuck Berry. We watched the concert from a field—sitting on the grass in the middle of five thousand French intellectuals and activists. Chuck Berry performed first, playing many of his big hits from the fifties and sixties including *Roll Over Beethoven*, *Johnny B Good* and *Maybelline*. The crowd loved it.

At the front of the audience were forty or fifty Dutch rock 'n roll fans dressed in leather jackets, blue jeans and T-shirts. They looked like they had just left a 1952 rock and roll party. But instead of sitting like the rest of the crowd, they stood up and started dancing to the music—enjoying themselves, but blocking the view of thousands of others who were seated on the grass field.

The crowd began chanting, *"Assiez, assiez, assiez"* (Sit down, sit down, sit down). Chuck Berry didn't seem to understand what the crowd was saying. I think he thought the chanting was some sort of verbal group hug for his music. The Dutch greasers ignored the crowd—but this was the wrong crowd for them to ignore. These five-thousand French men and women were the students, union activists and other political radicals who had manned the barricades and taken over the City of Paris in 1968.

The audience was becoming angrier and angrier. At the end of Chuck Berry's performance, Jerry Lee Lewis stepped onto the stage to start his high-energy act. By then, almost everyone in the audience was yelling *Assiez, assiez, assiez*. The tensions between the Dutch greasers and the French radicals were ready to explode. Just as Lewis started to perform, the situation it did blow up. A few young French radicals threw empty wine bottles at the Dutch greasers. Not to be outdone, the Dutch greasers returned those bottles— and added a few of their own.

The whole gathering turned into a riot. A member of Lewis' band was knocked unconscious. But the music kept coming. Jerry Lee actually stood on top of his piano as he continued to sing. Many in the audience were bleeding. Other festival attendees rushed from exhibition booths to join the brawl. The four of us moved to the outskirts of the melee. My friend was tightly gripping a wine bottle. He wanted to charge back into the center of the action and toss it. His French girlfriend talked him into putting it down. We left the festival.

Years later, I was in a tavern in Northfield, Minnesota drinking beer with some friends. Somebody put a quarter into a juke-box. A moment later, we heard the sounds of Chuck Berry singing *Johnny B Good* in concert. What I noticed, but my friends did not, was a chant in the background of the recording: *Assiez, assiez, assiez*.

I knew immediately when the recording had been made.

*****

In July, Swan Lake was performed in a courtyard of the Louvre. It starred the finest male and female ballet artists in the world, Rudolph Nureyev and Natalia

Makarova. They were defectors from Leningrad's Kirov Ballet who had never danced together. Free tickets were offered to the public. I was lucky enough to get a ticket to their second performance.

I was stunned by the elegance of Makarova— particularly by the graceful use of her hands as she danced the role of Odette, the swan. Her finesse was counter-balanced by the power and strength of Nureyev. The only disagreeable element in the first act of their performance was Japanese tourist photo flashbulbs continually interrupting the performance.

After an intermission, an announcement was made that another ballet artist would replace Nureyev for the rest of the performance. The audience didn't know what to make of it. The performance went on without the finest male ballet dancer in the world. Afterwards, I read in the Paris Herald Tribune that Makarova had been furious with what she considered to be the heavy-handed treatment she received from Nureyev during their duets. Their conflict during the performance made international news and Time Magazine covered it in an article the following week.

It was amazing to have witnessed such a sensational and controversial cultural event.

*****

I continued to enrich my life and improve my French by regularly attending films. French cinema was at the cutting edge of the movie making art form and Parisians were paying attention.

Films like *Valparaiso Valparaiso* (a wonderful comedy about a French intellectual and self-proclaimed radical who literally missed the boat to the Chilean revolution) and *Le Boucher*, (a psychological thriller by

Claude Chabrol) were topics of conversation among my friends at work. I also figured that discussing a controversial film would be a great icebreaker when and if I met a young woman as I walked through the Latin Quarter.

*****

Jean, a fellow resident at Hotel de la Renaissance was a student at the Sorbonne. Each weekend, he drove home to visit his family in rural Normandy. In early August, Jean invited me to join him for a weekend visit with his family. His parents owned and operated the only grocery store in a small village about an hour and a half north of Paris.

We drove to his home on a Saturday morning. Jean's family lived in an apartment above their grocery store. When we arrived at his parents' home, his mother was already beginning the evening meal. I remember sitting in her kitchen, watching her chop ingredients for a fish stew. I was amazed at the speed and precision with which she chopped the meal's ingredients. She displayed that level of skill during each step of our dinner's preparation.

After we ate, I sat down with Jean and his fifteen-year-old sister, a big fan of English rock and roll. She loved the Led Zeppelin's song *Stairway to Heaven*. But she had no idea what the lyrics meant. I had fun translating that enchanting song for her from English into French.

*****

Each Saturday morning, Madame Gaby and Monsieur Émile went to an open-air market to purchase ingredients for the meals Madame Gaby would prepare in the coming week. Since they did not have a car, one of our rue Poliveau neighbors drove them to the market. One Saturday, I was invited to join them.

We met at their restaurant at four in the morning, then drove to the market through the dark and quiet streets of a sleeping Paris. After parking the car, we walked through a large maze of booths and tents, each of which was crowded with displays of meats, baked goods, fresh fruit and vegetables, preserves or wines. Monsieur Émile and Madame Gaby were warmly greeted as friends by their food suppliers. These working-class vendors welcomed me and treated me graciously. Again and again, I was offered—and accepted—a piece of sausage, a slice of bread, or a wedge of cheese with a glass of wine or calvados.

We returned to rue Poliveau by seven that morning. I was more or less drunk. Since it was a Saturday morning, I was due at work at nine. I returned to bed and slept for an hour. When I awoke still inebriated, I went to a public phone and called into work. I had to take a sick day.

I had been welcomed into an open-air food market that had centuries of tradition—a place that very few Parisians or foreigners ever got to see. My wonderful friends, Monsieur Émile and Madame Gaby had shared with me a world that was truly magical—and that no longer exists.

*****

One weekend afternoon, as I walked through the Latin Quarter, I met a young American woman. After we spent an hour walking and talking, we were joined by a French man. The three of us continued our promenade. As we crossed a bridge over the Seine, the American woman said, "What would happen if I threw myself over the bridge into the river?"

The Frenchman responded without hesitating. "Ah yes, to die in Paris. That is a good death."

*****

Another time I was walking through the Latin Quarter on a Sunday evening with a young American woman. I could tell she hoped I would invite her to join me for dinner. And she attracted me. But unfortunately, it was Sunday afternoon at the end of the month and all of my resources had been spent. I had no money.

I recognized she would have had difficulty dealing with the fact that I couldn't afford to buy dinner for myself, let alone her. So, I told her I'd had a lovely time and wished her *au revoir*.

*****

I began one of my most special days in Paris in my room—depressed. It was an early Saturday afternoon. I was writing a letter to a friend telling him how sad I felt. All of a sudden, I felt ashamed. Here I was in the most wonderful city in the world and I was feeling sorry for myself because I had nothing to do. How could that be?

I pulled myself out of my malaise and went for a walk into an area of Paris I hadn't explored—the Marais, Paris' old Jewish quarter. It was a lovely walk and took me past the Place de la Bastille—the namesake of La Petite Bastille in Quebec—and through a couple of fascinating small historical museums. I ended up walking in the direction of the Louvre and found myself in a small but upscale art gallery. The woman who ran the gallery, Francoise, was about 30 years old. She had medium length, nicely coiffed, auburn hair, and was wearing an orange pastel silk blouse with white slacks.

The gallery displayed paintings by a contemporary Parisian painter. Francoise and I chatted in French about the artist and the gallery. She explained that the painter was *tres avant-garde* and highly regarded by the critics. I enjoyed the painter's colorful and whimsical abstract oil paint compositions.

Francoise told me that centuries before, the gallery had been a residence for members of the court of King Louis XIV. She offered to show me the cellar underneath the gallery that once had led to a passageway, long since sealed, and to the King's palace. We went down a circular stone stairway. The cellar and its vaulted ceilings seemed to be a part of another era of royal intrigues and secret passages.

Francoise told me that the artist whose paintings hung in the gallery occasionally hosted an event in that cellar chamber. He would paint a nude model while his guests—by invitation only—drank wine and listened to a small jazz combo. Francoise explained that only a few select guests were included. Then she invited me to a performance that evening.

I walked home that afternoon, aware that a sad day had turned into an adventure only because I had been willing to ignore my sadness and explore new avenues, so to speak.

I returned to the gallery that evening to attend the event. After being welcomed into the gallery by Francoise, I walked down the circular stone stairway to the cellar and heard the soft jazz sounds of a piano and string base. About fifteen guests were drinking glasses of red wine next to a nude model, a small tapped wooden cask of Côtes du Rhône and the artist. He was painting a work that tied together the evening's sights, sounds and atmosphere. From my perspective, his abstract painting had completely succeeded in recording the poetic atmosphere of the soiree.

The day had turned from one of my bluest Parisian days into one of my most satisfying. On a day that started out lonely, I had made a friend and expanded my experience in the City of Light.

Walking home that evening, I realized how very fortunate I was.

*****

One day at work, one of my colleagues suggested going out to lunch at the Rachmaninov Institute. I didn't know what that was. He explained to me that The Institute was a musical education center founded in Russia in the late 19th century. During the Russian revolution, the Rachmaninov Institute had moved permanently to Paris.

Five or six of us went to eat together that day. As I walked up to the old three-story brick building that housed the Institute, the sounds of piano, cello and oboe floated out of open windows confirming that the building was occupied by serious classical musicians. The restaurant in the basement of the Rachmaninov Institute was staffed by Russian emigres who had fled their motherland after Tsar Nicholas was deposed. The waiters—in their sixties and seventies—were dressed in clothing styles that predated the Tsar's overthrow.

I had a large lunch of borscht, pierogi, beef stroganoff, tea and vodka. For dessert, we shared small, beautiful and exotic petit fours soaked with brandy. The food was fabulous—its cost modest.

*****

Paris was a passionate environment of cultural richness that changed the way I viewed life. Every moment was fulfilling. I constantly was seeing and experiencing that richness—as I passed elegant shops on the *Champs-Elysées,* visited interesting museums or watched old men playing *boules* in the Parks. I found peace in seeing kids sail toy boats in the ponds of the *Jardin des Tuileries* and observing families and lovers walk through the elegant and dreamlike *Champs du Mars*, the large park in front of the Eiffel Tower.

I never took my time in Paris for granted. A special opportunity had been given to me. In the back of my mind, I could hear my sister Diane saying to me, "You are fortunate, Roger, to have this incredible opportunity."

I could almost hear her warning, "Don't waste it!"

*****

In early September 1973, I went to see Federico Fellini's film *La Dolce Vita*. The film's title literally means *The Sweet Life*. It was my first Fellini film and had a large impact on me. I left the theater recognizing that I needed to consider the film's message in the context of my own life.

Paris had been exciting and interesting. But I was visiting a culture that belonged to other people—one in which I was the outsider. It was suddenly clear to me that if I wanted to find meaning in my life, it must be within the context of my own culture. Richness from another culture that does not relate to one's inner self is like frosting without cake—a personal version of *La Dolce Vita*.

Instead of learning to appreciate how other people lived, it was time for me to establish roots—to create a life in my own culture. I recognized that somehow, I needed to find a way to earn a living in the United States—a living that had integrity and allowed me to be an integral part of a community. I needed to find friends in the U.S. and create the relationship with a woman that had, up to that point, eluded me.

*****

I gave these challenges a lot of thought. A strategy began to evolve. Now was the time to return to the United States—to Minnesota. But I needed to find a way to earn a living that would be satisfying and meaningful. I enjoyed working with my hands. I appreciated nature and hiking. What career would embrace those values?

After spending a week or so trying to answer that question, I came up with a plan. I would study forestry. I would pursue the education required to enter that field at the University of Minnesota. In so doing, I could live near family and friends. Once I had completed my studies, I would get a job as a forest ranger in rural Minnesota where I would build a life.

I shared my plan with my co-workers at the Council. Each person's response was kind and supportive.

A couple of days later, I gave Jack Egle my notice. I would leave the Council at the end of September.

*****

In the first week of October, 1973, I flew back to New York on a Council of Educational Exchange flight. Paris had been wonderful. But I was ready to build a life that had meaning.

14—Back to my Roots

My grandmother and grandfather had always been two of the most important people in my life. After my parents split up, their significance grew. During my college years, I visited them often. Their home becoming my personal retreat.

My grandfather had had a distinguished career in the restaurant industry. He began as a dishwasher in 1912 at the age of ten. By the time he retired in 1965, he was the most respected person in the Minnesota restaurant industry. But it was his integrity and demonstrated respect for others that won people's hearts.

My grandmother was known to her grandkids as *Bobbi*—our family's unique spelling of *Bubbe,* the Yiddish word for grandmother. When we were young, my cousins, sister, brother and I saw Bobbi as our own special Glinda, the Good Witch from *The Wizard of Oz.* Bobbi was always so kind and gentle to us munchkins.

Bobbi and Grandpa lived in a small three-bedroom North Minneapolis bungalow they purchased in 1940. Until I rented my own place, I would stay at their home.

*****

In the late 1930s, my grandparents took an orphan into their home. His name was Maurice. Maurice's life, before living with my grandparents, had been tough. His mother had had multiple nervous breakdowns and was placed in an asylum. His father had been an angry man who spent his days giving speeches in neighborhood parks criticizing the American government and proclaiming the success of socialism in the Soviet Union.

Between when Maurice moved in with my grandparents in 1938 and when I arrived in 1974, he had moved out twice. The first time was to fight in the Korean War. The second was when he married a woman named Jolene around 1960. That marriage had lasted a couple of years and produced no children. My cousins, my sister and I used to wish Maurice had stayed with Jolene.

Maurice was similar to Bluto, the *Popeye* comic book cartoon character. He was overweight, not to bright, bigoted, big mouthed and a bully. (Other than that, you might ask, how was the play?) Maurice's powerful hairy arms were covered with a serious skin rash that was obviously uncomfortable. He often scratched his arms, drawing blood and leaving scabs. His thick black greased-back hair (the rage in the early 1950s) had turned gray by 1973—but it was still greased back.

When I arrived from Paris, Maurice had already been unemployed for more than a decade. He had had once been a railroad engineer. But in 1963, when the Northern Pacific Railway had negotiated reductions in staffing with the Railway Workers' Union, Maurice had been shrewd enough to accept a buyout of his seniority and pension. That lump sum payment provided enough funds for Maurice to purchase an almost new Buick Electra.

*****

My grandparents had had two daughters, but no sons. Until I was born, Maurice felt he was as close as my grandparents had to a son. My birth changed that. Perhaps that was the reason that he never liked me too much. When I was a college student visiting my grandparents, Maurice would threaten to cut my hair while I slept. He tried to discuss Vietnam with me in the late 1960s. Recognizing his unique intellect and ability to approach things in a rational manner, I avoided any political discussions with him.

It seemed like my grandmother enjoyed the drama Maurice brought into their home. Over the years, he caused many arguments between my grandfather and her. But when Maurice created too much excitement, my grandmother was able to stop him. If absolutely necessary, she would cry. After she had cried and Maurice had been chastised for creating a scene, he would silently and gruffly return to his room in the unfinished basement.

*****

An excellent example of that drama occurred shortly after I arrived from Paris. My grandmother had made waffles for breakfast that morning. I was putting butter and sugar on my waffles.

Maurice told me in his rough blutoesque manner, "Sugar is bad for you and you shouldn't be putting it on those waffles."

He went on and on, refusing to stop. I tried to ignore his comments. Finally, my grandmother had had enough.

With great passion, she said, "Maurice. Look at your waffle. You have powdered sugar on it that's half an inch deep! How come that's okay but Roger can't put some regular sugar onto his?"

Maurice paused for a moment, a little taken back. Then, in his typical gruff voice, he said, "Well, uhm—when they—uh—grind the regular sugar into powdered sugar, they—uhm—they destroy all the bad things in it."

How can one respond to such a brilliant argument?

*****

Before I graduated, I sold most of my possessions. By combining the proceeds of those sales with cash graduation gifts and my other savings, I was able to put enough money into a savings account to fund my college loan payments while I traveled.

Since I was going to rent an apartment, have a job, attend university, and visit my relatives, I needed a car. I opted to use some of my savings to purchase it. I considered buying a new car. The amount I had in savings, more than two thousand dollars, would pay the full cost for a new Volkswagen Beetle. However, I decided it would be more prudent to keep those savings to apply to my college loans. I would buy a used car.

Maurice offered to help me find a car. He knew a lot more about cars than I did and, since I would need rides to see cars, it seemed like an offer I should accept. As I have pointed out, I always thought everything through thoroughly.

Maurice thought I should buy a car like his Buick Electra. It was nineteen feet of steel, chrome and luxury. Ok, maybe it only got seven miles per gallon. But miles per gallon wasn't an issue for Maurice since he had nowhere to go. In any case, I wasn't about to buy a big old boat like Maurice's Buick.

*****

Each time we went to look at a car, Maurice interrogated the seller with the purpose of finding the vehicle's major hidden faults. The only time Maurice did encourage me to purchase a car was at his friend's used car lot. According to Maurice, all of the vehicles in that small lot were incredible values despite the fact that they were high mileage, their engines were covered with dirt and oil and they had rusted bodies. I held little difficulty holding myself back from jumping at those opportunities.

On Saturday mornings, Maurice would visit his one buddy. One Saturday morning, right after Maurice had left the house, I reviewed the Minneapolis Star used car ads. There it was, a 1967 Dodge Dart. Its owner was asking only three-hundred and fifty dollars—and I knew that Darts were good cars. I called the owner and was relieved to find out that his car hadn't been sold yet. I quizzed him on the vehicle. He told me it ran well. What a deal!

My grandfather lent me his car and I drove off to check out the Dodge Dart.

*****

The car looked good. Its five-digit odometer showed 65,000 miles. I was eager to go for a test drive. The car's owner volunteered to drive. Evidently, having him test drive the Dart must have seemed like a good idea at the time, because I agreed.

The car behaved pretty well for him during the test drive. After that, I kicked the tires and inspected the car's body. It probably was going to need a paint job and maybe a few other improvements. But, for that price, how could I go wrong?

I wrote the check—no sense in quibbling over price on such a good deal. Since I had to drive my grandfather's car back to my grandparents' home, the seller graciously offered to follow me in my newly purchased 1967 Dodge Dart. His sister followed him in her car. Once we arrived at my grandparents' home, the former car owner and his sister got out of Dodge, so to speak.

I spent the next seven months learning how many things can go wrong with a three-hundred-and-fifty-dollar car even if it only had 65,000 miles—or maybe that was 165,000—or was it 265,000? But I don't want to get too far ahead on that story. Needless to say, Maurice was not impressed with my purchase. From that point forward, he often entertained himself by voicing his perspectives on my car-buying skills.

And oh, by the way, if I ever need to write a tutorial about how *not* to buy a car, I have completed my research. I am ready to go.

*****

In order to become a forester, I needed to complete a degree in forestry. A University of Minnesota admissions officer advised me to take several courses prior to applying for admission to the University Master's Program in Forestry. Since it was too late to enroll for fall term, I would take those courses in the winter and spring quarters. Then I could apply in late spring for admission to the Master's Program starting in fall of the coming year.

*****

My next challenge was to find a job. By that point, I had sufficient blue collar working experience and skills. But in addition to that, my low-paying job interview technique had almost become an art form—and now, I actually intended to get a Master's.

Within a couple of days, I secured employment as a janitor at St. Paul's Children's Hospital. I would work from three-thirty in the afternoon until midnight Mondays through Fridays. The swing-shift would allow me to take classes at the University during the day and I would have weekends off.

Things were going well.

*****

I chose to look for an apartment in St. Paul rather than in Minneapolis. It would be closer to my new job and the University. Many St. Paul neighborhoods were full of vintage craftsman homes on boulevards canopied with large old elms. I hoped to find a place in one of those classic neighborhood homes.

And luck was running with me. I quickly found a third-floor gabled attic apartment in a lovely old Victorian house. The home's owner had lived there for all of her seventy-five years. The apartment included a kitchen, a living room, a small bathroom, a bedroom and a second unheated bedroom. It was simply furnished, had a private entrance off of a wooden staircase attached to the back of the home and its rent was only sixty-five dollars a month.

My plan was coming together. I had a car. I had a job. I had an apartment. Soon, I would be working on a forestry degree. And for the first time since I had graduated from college, I had family and friends living near me.

My life seemed pretty full.

*****

I started working at Children's Hospital during the first week of November of 1973. My job included a variety of repetitive cleaning tasks as well as other occasional support for nursing staff. My regular tasks took about two hours from each work shift.

Our swing-shift crew was made up of four janitorial staff. In addition to myself, there were two women—both named Audrey—and a guy named Joey. Both Audreys had teen-age children. Audrey number one was in her mid-fifties and had a well sprayed blonde beehive hairdo. She was thin, wore a short tight fitting maid's uniform and was extremely confident.

Audrey number two had mousy blond hair with a 1950s tightly curled permanent. She was about the same age as Audrey number one, but not as thin, coiffed or confident. Audrey number two wore an outfit similar to Audrey number one, but in a larger size. It was clear from the outset. Audrey number one ran the show and Audrey number two was her side-kick.

Joey was a nice guy. As the other male janitor, he trained me for all my regular tasks.

The swing-shift crew also included a maintenance engineer position for which staffing rotated among four men who took turns covering the hospital's day, night and swing-shifts.

Our crew worked well together. But neither Joey nor any of the engineers ever crossed the Audreys.

*****

My work routine was simple. For the first two hours, I emptied wastebaskets, waxed floors and vacuumed carpets. Then, as I quickly discovered, the janitorial crew spent most of their time in the break room playing poker. As a member of the janitorial team, I was expected to do the same. A maintenance engineer sometimes joined our game.

The poker game required no skill. It was a simplified version of five-card-draw. The ante for each hand was twenty-five cents. After receiving five cards, each player could discard and draw up to four cards, but they had to bet a second twenty-five cents for that privilege. No other betting occurred. No other variables existed. Once each player who had bet the second twenty-five cents had drawn their cards, everyone showed their hands. Whoever had the best hand won the pot.

While we sat in the little housekeeping room playing cards, we talked. Audrey number one would tell us about the world. Her husband was a truck driver—and truck drivers—

well, truck drivers understand a lot of things. So, Audrey number 1 not only had the advantage of having a lot of insight into everything herself, but she could share her husband's vast knowledge as well. The rest of us were allowed to offer an occasional perspective, but Audrey number one knew a lot and dominated all conversations.

I had rarely played poker. But passing time playing cards seemed okay. Since there was no skill involved in the game, one would expect the winnings to even out. Right?

My bad luck was that I was lucky. I consistently was dealt good cards. I started winning about four or five dollars a night. It took only a few days before the Audreys believed I might be cheating. I am not sure how one could cheat in this idiot-proof form of poker. But they were concerned I was doing it. So, being a realist, I decided I was better off not playing poker.

Bad idea.

Now the Audreys felt I was stuck up because I *didn't* play poker.

*****

Each Saturday morning, I visited my grandparents. I had a key to their North Minneapolis home and arrived at eight. My grandparents were still sleeping. I went quietly into their kitchen where I made biscuits from scratch, orange juice from frozen concentrate, and a pot of Folgers coffee in an old, beat-up, aluminum stove-top percolator. At nine, my grandparents came downstairs from their bedroom. The coffee and orange juice had been poured, biscuits were almost out of the oven and the table had been set with dishes, silverware, cream, sugar, butter and strawberry jelly.

Breakfast with my grandparents was the beginning of a wonderful Saturday ritual. After eating, we adjourned to their living room couch. I would sit between my grandmother and grandfather as we paged through old photo albums. Every photograph had a story behind it. There were pictures of the Buick they drove in the early 1930s to visit Bobbi's folks at their modest farm in Wisconsin. When Bobbi saw that old roadster and its rumble seat trunk, she'd tell me about the picnic she and my grandfather had with my mother and Auntie Joyce at a northern Wisconsin roadside park. When my grandfather saw a picture of Neil Messick and his wife taken in the fifties at the Nicollet Hotel's Waikiki Room, he reminisced about the trip he and Neil had taken to Chicago in 1958. Bobbi would point to a 1940s photo of a chef standing in front of a display of food. She would shake her head and say, "That's Oscar Braun. He passed away a couple years ago. What a shame. He was still such a young man."

I remember those tours through their memories as if my grandfather and grandmother had shared them with me yesterday. The time I spent with them on that couch is irreplaceable. Their recollections continue to enrich my life.

*****

After viewing photo albums for half an hour, my grandfather and I would leave to go play pool at the Shriners Lodge. We would travel there in my car—I was so proud of it. The Shriners Lodge was a beautiful old mansion on a street shaded by large stately elms. It was in a Minneapolis neighborhood full of grand Victorian and Prairie Style homes

Grandpa—that's what I called him—and I would enter the Shriners Lodge through an impressive front room.

The aura of the entire lodge was expressed clearly by that room's stained-glass windows, large dark oriental carpets and plush overstuffed furniture—a complete set from another era. My grandfather and I would walk through a mahogany paneled hallway; then go down a stairway to the billiards room. Its décor couldn't have changed much in the prior fifty years. It was furnished with large leather chairs and three ornate pool tables. Its walls were covered with pool cue racks and old paintings.

*****

Pool was the only game—other than gin rummy—that I ever saw my grandfather play. As a young man, he worked a split shift for decades. During his three-hour midday break, he walked to a nearby downtown billiard hall where he played pool.

While we played, Grandpa would pause to accuse me of being a pool shark (even though he was letting me win). After four or five games of eight-ball, we would retire to the Shriners Café located on the main floor of the turn-of-the-century mansion.

We each ordered a hot corn beef on rye sandwich with a cup of coffee. The rye bread was always fresh. The sandwich had a ton of delicate and thinly sliced corn beef. There was also a scoop of potato salad on the plate as well as a large kosher dill pickle. We spooned French's yellow mustard onto the side of our plates so that each bite of our sandwiches could be bathed in mustard. Then, Grandpa and I would sit there, drinking our coffee; he with cream and sugar; me with just cream.

Then he would tell me more stories about his career and share other memories. He would talk about his values; telling me that when he ran the catering and the restaurants at the Nicollet Hotel, other executives expected him to eat in the executive staff dining room. But he never ate there. He ate with his staff in the regular employee lunchroom. My grandfather had been a good boss and was loved by his employees. As we sat there, he was teaching me lessons about life.

Grandpa shared memories of people he had known. For example, when prohibition ended, there were rumors that he would become the first commissioner of liquor for the state of Minnesota. He was invited to meet with the Governor Floyd B. Olsen to discuss the position. But before he arrived for the interview, Governor Olsen had offered the position to someone else. The governor saved face by offering my grandfather a job as a laborer on a highway crew.

Thanks a lot!

*****

My grandfather told me about an unusual conversation at a hotel banquet in 1952. The manager of a large Twin Cities Chevrolet dealership had drunk too much. He asked my grandfather what sort of car he drove. My grandfather told him he had a '46 Chevy. The car dealer told my grandfather to bring his car into the dealership that Monday. "I'll give you a brand-new Chevrolet in exchange."

Monday morning, my grandfather called the automobile dealer and asked him if he remembered the conversation. The dealer said of course, he remembered it. He said that if my grandfather brought his old Chevy into the dealership that day, he'd drive off in a new car—at no cost.

My grandfather brought his car into the dealership. A couple of hours later, he drove off in a spiffy yellow and gray 1952 Chevrolet Bel Air Coupe. Grandpa concluded that story by adding that unfortunately, the dealer was fired the next day.

*****

One conversation I had with my grandfather at the Shriners was pretty poignant. "There was a time, Roger, when everybody who was anybody in this town owed me a favor. But it was not my style to collect on those favors." My grandfather puffed on his cigar after saying that. Then he continued, "Now, they're all dead, Roger. And nobody remembers those stories." He paused again before completing his thought. "Nobody remembers me."

And I think it was the truth. In 1973, my grandfather and grandmother were living on the edge of poverty. But in 1964, Hubert Humphrey invited my grandparents to the presidential inauguration of Lyndon Johnson. My grandmother had poured at an inaugural tea with Lady Bird Johnson.

I guess the moral here is that as time passes, things change.

*****

After my grandfather had paid for our lunch, we would return to the pool hall. He would take out a couple of cigars and hand me one. We would smoke our cigars as we played our final game of eight-ball. At the end of that game, I would drive us back to my grandparents. I'd go into their home, say goodbye to my grandmother and thank my grandfather one more time for buying me lunch. Then I'd take off.

But sometimes, after my grandfather and I had returned from playing eight-ball, I would sit down for another half an hour with my grandmother. Bobbi was a deeply passionate person with a brilliant sense of humor. I loved to sit at the dining room table with her, drinking coffee and listening to her stories about growing up in a log cabin in northern Wisconsin.

Bobbi's family had been poor. Her father had raised a couple of milk cows and worked as a logger. But her memories of growing up in that log cabin in the wilderness were joyful. She was able to share wonderful stories from throughout her life—accompanying each tale with joy, humor or sadness that made it memorable. Anyone who knew my grandmother came to appreciate her genius in telling these beautiful stories.

*****

For my grandparents, having company meant sharing their table with a slew of relatives—and putting up with a lot of chaos. At those gatherings, my Bobbi and Grandpa often quibbled between themselves. After hearing them, some people thought my grandparents didn't get along so well. I knew from those wonderful Saturdays that their respect and tenderness for one another was ongoing. My grandfather would often say during our Shriner lunches, "Your Bobbi is such a beautiful woman."

And my grandmother would always treat my grandfather with the same level of gentle kindness and respect. Being with them—witnessing their affection for one another—was a lesson in the love and respect a married couple should have for one another.

*****

The first event I attended after graduating from college was Jim and Liz's wedding. Jim attended Carleton with me while Liz had been a student at the University of Minnesota. Now that I lived in the Twin Cities, my friendship with them was central in my life. We would get together almost every weekend, go for a drive, watch a movie, make a film or cook a delightful meal. Jim and Liz had a zest for life that regularly propelled them into exploring new things with their whole hearts. We went cross-country skiing, dined at unusual restaurants, prepared Indian food, and attended jazz and blues concerts. And sometimes, we just got stoned, made up funny stories and laughed.

In 1974, Jim and Liz were both finishing medical school at the University of Minnesota. They were each passionate about medicine. But the two of them faced different challenges in their medical education.

Sexism was common at the University's Medical School. The school not only accepted far fewer women than men students, but those women medical students ran a gauntlet of disrespect while completing their educations. Liz constantly was faced with shabby treatment and sexist attitudes from professors and fellow students. Her courage and integrity in dealing with those challenges inspired my respect.

*****

As a Christmas gift, I gave Jim and Liz a bottle of 1961 Château Lafitte Rothschild. The bottle cost thirty-one dollars, a small fortune in 1973. I have since learned that the '61 Lafitte was one of the great vintages of the 20th century.

After I gave them the bottle, we went to a small Italian restaurant to eat spaghetti and drink the wine. The waitress informed us that she could not serve a customer's bottle at the table. She offered to decant it and bring the wine to the table in a carafe. As we waited for the decanted wine, we laughed and mused—how would we know if the waitress had switched bottles and instead served us a cheap wine? When the decanter arrived, I learned what the term *bouquet* means. The aroma of the wine was so rich, so thick, that even as the wine sat in its decanter, you could almost touch its complex aroma—as if it was a bouquet of flowers!

*****

Sometimes, Jim and I made plans for lunch or a game of squash and Liz was not included. One evening following a squash game with Jim, Liz was especially cold to me. I asked her what was wrong. At first, she denied that there was a problem. I kept pushing. Finally, she told me that she was tired of being a second-class friend. It seemed to her like I had a close relationship with her husband, but I treated her as a tag-along. She said she didn't need that sort of friend.

After listening to her, I could see why she felt badly. So, I asked Liz to go out to dinner and a movie. She responded warmly. We had a wonderful meal of matzo ball soup and blintzes at the Lincoln Delicatessen, a quality Jewish deli that my aunt and uncle had patronized for decades. Afterwards, Liz and I saw the film *The Great Gatsby*. We closed our evening by going out for dessert and talking about *Gatsby*, other films we had seen—and about our friendship.

That was the only time that Liz and I went out without Jim. It enriched our friendship. The understanding created that evening increased the trust among all three of us.

*****

Inspired by my recollection of Solomon Smith's family barbecues, I invited Jim and Liz to a dinner of home-cooked barbecue ribs. I wanted the meal to be special. So, I asked Bobbi how to cook ribs. She recommended I use beef instead of pork and bake the ribs before putting any sauce on them. Then I should bathe them in my barbecue sauce and bake them again until they looked ready to serve.

That sounded like a plan to me. I headed for the grocery store. The store's butcher helped me select some nice beef short ribs. But I didn't have a recipe for barbecue sauce. I recalled that Solomon Smith's family picnics utilized tomato sauce, brown sugar and vinegar as a base for the sauce. But I had no idea what spices or special ingredients to add to that base.

I came up with a wonderful strategy. I walked around the grocery store, asking for advice from each woman who looked like she was a good cook regarding what ingredients I should add to my barbecue sauce. As I walked up to a conscripted expert, I would tell her, "I'm going to make barbecue ribs for my friends. You look like a good cook. What would you recommend that I put in my barbecue sauce—in addition to tomato sauce, brown sugar and vinegar?"

After giving an initial look of discomfort at being approached by a stranger with long hair, each of my experts bought into my approach. She would start out by confirming I had shown good judgment by asking for her opinion. Then she would give her list of recommended additives. I thanked each coach, bought all of their recommended ingredients, and returned home to prepare dinner. Their cumulative suggestions included soy sauce, ginger, dry mustard, pineapple juice, garlic, cayenne pepper, onions, parsley, oregano, olive oil, salt, pepper, Tabasco, lemon juice, cloves and a few other ingredients I no longer recall.

I've not since used that method for developing a recipe. But it worked well and the ribs were fantastic. I have continued to make barbecue ribs from time to time and no one has ever complained about the sauce.

*****

Karen and I were back in touch with one another sending letters full of hope and memories back and forth. It culminated in a visit by Karen from Chicago for a long New Year's Eve weekend. Karen and I double-dated with Jim and Liz; going to a fabulous New Year's Eve party that featured a big band and an incredible buffet. After dancing, drinking and laughing our way through the chaotic celebratory event, we were totally drunk—at least I was. I often think (with a great deal of shame) about that drive home. I tried to drive carefully as I weaved my way home avoiding all major thoroughfares; staying on icy back-roads. But it wasn't safe. I shouldn't have been behind the wheel.

Jim and Liz spent the night in my small second bedroom. The next morning, I made a wonderful breakfast of curried scrambled eggs, peach melba, fresh biscuits and coffee served with an orange juice and white wine spritzer. What a breakfast!

The visit with Karen was sheer joy. But the distance between Chicago and Minneapolis—more metaphorical than actual—was too great. As the weeks after the visit passed, it became clear to both of us that our love relationship was not destined to last.

*****

I enrolled at the University of Minnesota in January of 1974. I was taking a couple of courses required to enter their master's in forestry program. I hadn't studied economics at Carleton and had failed my only biology class.

222

I was confident I would excel in these two courses with my improved attitude and fresh resolve.

The economics course was intriguing. In the past, I had heard references to economic allocation dynamics regarding the choice between guns and butter. But it had always seemed like an odd set of alternatives. Shouldn't you decide that before you go to a store? After our instructor explained the concept of an economy's finite capacity to invest, I came to understand the relationship between these two unrelated, but symbolic items.

I have repressed my memory of the biology course. But I studied hard and was learning what I needed to learn in order to pass the course. However, taking the course confirmed that I had made a wise decision in not pursuing a medical degree.

Attending classes with students who were four or five years younger than me was interesting. I met some attractive young coeds. But they seemed like kids.

*****

Being a thorough planner, I took the time to check out the forest ranger job market. The federal and state governments were the primary employers of forest rangers. I checked with those agencies and found out there were not a lot of job openings. Too many baby boomers had already gotten degrees in forestry and, as a result, there was intense competition for the few positions that were vacant. It was going to be harder to get a job as a forest ranger than, for example, a position as a janitor in a hospital. I learned my fantasy of earning a living walking in the woods and being at peace with myself and nature—well, it might not be easy to achieve. After getting a master's degree, I might not be able to find a job.

The good news was that after three weeks of classes, I was confident I could pass the courses in which I had enrolled. The bad news was that I didn't like studying any more than I had as an undergraduate and I'd lost confidence that my studies would lead to the career I sought. If I quit the University immediately, I could get all of my tuition back. So, three weeks after enrolling at the University, I withdrew and my efforts to become a forest ranger had ceased.

*****

An interesting dynamic at St. Paul's Children's Hospital was its workers' class system. Doctors were the metaphorical titled gentry class. Registered nurses were one step down—but a large step. Licensed practical nurses were a step below registered nurses. X-ray and laboratory technicians were one additional step down this theoretical social structure ladder.

At the bottom of the hierarchy were the maintenance employees. They were divided into several layers, the highest of which was engineers; then came landscaping staff; and kitchen and janitorial staff were the bottom of the food chain. Administrative staff of all levels appeared to be fairly irrelevant to actual work done at a hospital.

Detroit's Grace Hospital had no similar hierarchy. I think that might have been because so many of the employees at Grace were people of color. They had learned better than to judge a person because of his or her rank within an organization. The employees at Grace Hospital in Detroit didn't have the artificial walls of arrogance and disrespect that were so prevalent within our small St. Paul hospital.

The Children's Hospital class system only bothered me in one regard—attractive nurses would not demean themselves by talking to a janitor. An available attractive nurse wanted to meet somebody who aspired to some level of success; someone who would someday provide them with the meaningful level of social and economic security they deserved.

As a janitor, I had no prospects. So, few nurses chose to speak with me. Why would they? I couldn't offer them what they sought. The fact that I had a college degree from the most prestigious college in the state might have caused some to reconsider. But they didn't know that about me and rarely spoke to me. After all, I was a janitor. What would have been the point?

My perspective was that anyone that superficial was not worth knowing.

Of course, a couple of nurses were exceptions. They were very cool—attractive—and fun to speak with—but married.

*****

A pleasant and meaningful part of my job at Children's was spending time with our young patients. I got to know a couple of kids quite well. One of them was a two-and-a-half-year-old boy who had a serious liver disease called biliary atresia. At the time, the illness had no cure. Brendan weighed about 20 pounds and was the size of a one-year-old. His skin was yellow. But there was so much sweetness in him. Brendan was always sad. I never saw him smile. No family ever visited him. He virtually became a child of the hospital.

Brendan was destined to die in the hospital without any of the special love from others that he deserved. I enjoyed spending time at his bedside.

I will never forget his deep, soulful and sad eyes.

*****

I became close to one other child patient. Michael was about four years old. He suffered from a severe case of autism. Like Brendan, he was rarely visited by family members. Michael didn't ever speak. But, his subtle awareness of others—when they chose to give him attention—was endearing. I sometimes stood next to the high chair in which he spent most of each day and let him hold my pocket watch. On the watch's face were colorful illustrations of cows, flowers and farmers. As he held the watch in his little hands, Michael would get lost in its illustrations. One time, after visiting him for about fifteen minutes, I told him that I needed to return to my duties.

Michael, who never made eye contact or gave any indication that he heard or understood anything, had been intensely studying my watch. When I told him I needed to leave, he promptly threw my watch to the floor. Fortunately, it didn't break. But this act informed me that his awareness was much greater than I had understood.

I am sure the loneliness Michael carried within him was beyond anything that I could fathom.

*****

One of the funniest things I ever saw in any workplace occurred one winter evening at St. Paul Children's. The temperature had increased above freezing— rare for St. Paul in January. Then, after a light rain, the temperature dropped back to the low twenties and the pavement turned to ice. This was followed by a light snowfall.

Children's Hospital was located at the top of a steep hill. Its driveway had a sharp incline. Its parking lot was located next to that driveway. That evening, as visitors pulled out of the parking lot onto the driveway, their cars just slid down the hill, colliding with other vehicles along the way. Soon there were seven or eight damaged vehicles at the bottom of a steep driveway.

Tom, a junior maintenance engineer, arrived at the hospital to address this situation. Tom was enthusiastic, straightforward and young. He knew he needed to spread a layer of sand on the driveway as soon as possible. He quickly put tire chains on the hospital's four-wheel-drive truck, loaded sand onto its bed and started down the driveway—from the top of the hill.

Through a window overlooking the parking lot and driveway, a group of us had been entertained by the series of collisions that had already occurred. But as Tom pulled out onto the driveway, we were about to see the *coup de grâce*. As his truck turned onto the driveway, it began to slide. And as it slid down the hill, it moved faster and faster. Before coming to a stop, Tom's truck had hit every one of the cars at the bottom of that hill.

Fortunately, no one was hurt.

We would never have laughed to Tom's face. But as the truck skated down the hill, nailing one vehicle after another, we roared.

*****

Living in the Twin Cities gave me an opportunity to spend time with my Aunt Joyce, Uncle Harold and their five daughters. My aunt and uncle had always welcomed me into their home. There was always good food to eat and plenty of television football to watch.

Harold and Joyce had taught me about what a family can be. They loved their daughters and they loved one another. Harold's focus on family was a model for how a father can hold a family together.

During that winter of '73-'74, I spent time with each of my cousins and enjoyed other Twin Cities relatives including an aunt and uncle who ran the best delicatessen in St. Paul—*Cecil's*. I loved living near so many relatives.

*****

Uncle Harold had a tough childhood. He quit school in the seventh grade to support his family. Later, after already being madly in love with my Aunt Joyce, he joined the military, went to Europe and fought heroically in World War II.

Harold fought in the Battle of the Bulge. He told the story that on a cold snowy night, while German artillery bombardment landed non-stop around his company, he told his men, "Anybody who lives through the night gets pancakes for breakfast".

While this is wonderful story, Harold was known to embellish and my mom had doubts about the accuracy of the story. However, in 1963, my mom was discussing the Battle of the Bulge with a veteran seated next to her on an airline flight. The man shared a story about seeing "a passionate Jewish sergeant walking around a Belgian Village on a morning during the Battle of the Bulge. The sergeant was asking just about everyone he ran into if they knew where he could get some baking powder for pancakes."

Harold was seriously wounded several times during the war. When he returned to the United States, the use of his arms was limited. He became the sales manager for a shoe store. Each night, Harold would bring home the store's accounting ledgers to complete balancing the day's sales. In reality, Harold was unable to make the entries into the ledgers because of injuries to his arms. Each night, my Aunt Joyce did the accounting for the prior day's sales.

*****

My Dodge Dart was nickel-and-diming me to death. It had begun fairly inauspiciously. I decided to install a rear radio speaker. Once it was installed, I felt like my car was complete. Unfortunately, I blew the speaker out by turning the volume up too much while listening to Gordon Lightfoot's song *Sundown*. That was an easy and inexpensive fix. I just purchased and installed another speaker. Other repair projects turned out to be a bit more complex.

I was having difficulty changing gears on the Dart. So, I had the clutch replaced. After a flat tire, I discovered my tires were bald and had to replace all four tires. The paint on the Dart was peeling. So, I had the car painted a beautiful shade of light blue. (Note to self: Cheap paint jobs won't last).

But the car's biggest problem was that it burned a lot of oil. I soon learned that was because my engine was shot. I priced out replacing the car's motor and discovered it would be quite expensive—more than I could afford. At that point, I was still taking classes at the University. A classmate told me replacing a car engine was pretty easy. He would help me do it. That sounded too good to pass up.

It was January, a cold time in Minnesota to work outdoors on a car. I asked my aunt and uncle if I could replace the engine in my car in their garage. Harold and

Joyce were a little taken back, but they were generous and told me I could.

My classmate helped me select a rebuilt engine and the many other parts I would need to replace once I got the old engine out of my Dart. We used his truck to pick up the rebuilt engine and he lent me a few necessary tools to get the job done. I rented the others.

My mechanical adventure had just begun. The first day went pretty well. We got the old engine out and placed the rebuilt engine in the car—but had not yet hooked it up in any way. Our plan was to do that the following day. Unfortunately, my classmate had a family emergency. He called me that evening to tell me he couldn't help anymore. I could use his tools, but I would have to depend fully on the *Haynes Repair 1967 Dodge Dart Service Manual* I purchased at the auto parts store.

I didn't have a clue what I was doing. Again and again, I would install a part, only to discover I'd done it incorrectly or in the wrong sequence. I would pull the part out—then reinstall it later—correctly—in the right sequence. I made constant trips back forth to the auto parts store investing in additional auto parts.

My tenacity was driven by quiet desperation. There is no feeling as helpless as taking apart something upon which you depend, then discovering you do not know how to put it back together. I ended up taking a week's vacation in order to work on my car. By the end of the week, I had the motor running—well enough to drive the car into an auto repair shop. There, I paid an auto mechanic to fix my mistakes.

By the time the installation was complete—read this as *repaired by the auto repair shop*—the car ran beautifully.

I had learned a lot. I was even able to set the timing on the engine by ear. My Dart was getting good mileage. After I paid to have its muffler replaced, it ran so quietly that you couldn't hear the engine purr even when you stood right next to it. I was so proud!

Of course, it cost quite a bit. By the time I was done, my total investment into that Dodge Dart was greater than the purchase price would have been for a brand-new Volkswagen Beetle. I have often described my experience working on the Dart as the cheapest MBA available.

Fixing that car taught me the principles of capital investment including, sunk costs, project planning and risk management.

*****

In the spring of my junior year of college, I was one of a group of students who regularly went horse riding at a farm near the college. The farm was situated next to a couple hundred forested acres. It had about thirty horses. The farmer charged each of us one dollar for an hour's ride.

Other students with whom I had gone horse riding graduated in 1970. Each weekday in April and May of 1971, I used a college car to drive five or six other students out to the farm to go horse riding. The farmer was so pleased I was bringing paying riders that he allowed me to ride for free. I rode bareback on a stallion Palomino quarter horse named Dandy.

In the spring of 1974, I returned to the farm to go horse riding with Jim and Liz. The farmer welcomed me and we had a wonderful ride. Afterwards, the farmer showed me a colt named Marco that Dandy had sired. Marco was a large, muscular dark chestnut. He had never been ridden— he wouldn't even let anyone come near to him. I asked the farmer if I could try to tame Marco—then try to ride him. The farmer was thrilled somebody was willing to take that on and quickly said *yes*.

In April and May, I drove down to the farm once a week to spend time with Marco. At first, the young stallion wouldn't even let me touch him. As time passed, he came to trust me. One week, I discovered a four-inch nail had pierced Marco's hoof. I patiently and carefully removed the nail. The farmer was amazed that Marco trusted me enough to let me remove it. The horse's trust for me had leaped forward.

Each week, I made progress. By mid-May, I was at a point where Marco allowed me to put a saddle and bridle on him.

*****

My brother Johnny's bar mitzvah was scheduled for June in Denver. I would attend.

I did not have a lot of reasons to return to the Twin Cities after the bar mitzvah. I had failed to create a career in the Twin Cities—and had not found the love of my life. I told my family and friends I would not return to Minneapolis-St. Paul. I also gave notice to Children's Hospital.

I did not know what was next. I just knew I had not yet found my path.

*****

The day before I left the Twin Cities, I visited Marco. I told the farmer I was moving away; that this would be my last visit with the big dark chestnut and I wanted to try to ride Marco that morning. The farmer thanked me for my efforts and wished me luck. His wife and children joined him in the barnyard to watch whatever was about to occur.

I put a saddle and bridle on Marco. Speaking softly to the already nervous horse, I told him what I was going to do, why I was going to do it. Then, I slowly put my foot into the stirrup and got onto his back. Marco just stood there—not moving. While that was progress, given that it was my last visit, I needed to push things further. I gave a light kick into his sides. Marco took off running, jumping and bucking. I stayed on his back for about half a minute, ending up on the ground, slightly humiliated, but unharmed.

I wasn't done. I brushed myself off and got back onto Marco. Again, when prompted by me, Marco ran and jumped around the barnyard for a couple of minutes. But this time I didn't fall off. Finally, Marco stopped. He stood calmly. I figured that was about as good as it was going to get. I slowly stepped down from the saddle, gave Marco some kind words and a carrot, took off the saddle, then the bridal and rubbed the still nervous horse down.

Then, I said goodbye.

My attempt to ride Marco is an excellent metaphor for my efforts to find a home over the prior few years. While I kept ending up on the ground, I continually climbed back into the saddle—taking another shot—hoping for success.

*****

The next day, I was off to Denver to celebrate my brother's bar mitzvah. I packed my belongings into the Dart and said goodbye to friends and family. I would see my grandparents, cousins, uncles and aunts in Denver. Still, saying goodbye to the Twin Cities was tough. My hopes had not turned into my accomplishments.

It had been a good nine months. But I was once again on the road.

15—Moving On

The high school I attended in Moorhead was a part of the college where my dad was president. While my parents' separation was fascinating gossip for many, it was of particular interest to my high school teachers. My dad was their boss. To put it mildly, my high school experience had become uncomfortable.

As dysfunction took over my family home, I separated myself from most of my friends at school. During those high school years, I was fortunate to have a special friend, Laura. Laura played the clarinet, acted in school plays, enjoyed tennis and lived fully. Most importantly for me, she was a kind person and a good friend. We didn't talk about the chaos occurring in my home. But Laura was well aware of it. As I look back at our friendship, what stands out most was our ability to laugh together.

Unfortunately, during my sophomore year—her junior year—Laura got pregnant. The child's father was a student teacher. In February, Laura dropped out of school. I was devastated. In addition to absorbing conflict in my home and having separated from most of my classmates, I had lost my best friend.

*****

Several weeks before I left St. Paul, I learned that Laura was living in southern Minnesota with her husband and two children. We wrote to one another and set up a plan for me to visit Laura on my way to Denver. Once I'd said goodbye to friends and family in the Twin Cities, I headed south, spending an hour and a half driving to the small town in which Laura lived.

I pulled into the driveway of her home at mid-morning. It was warm and sunny. Laura and I went for a walk. We talked about our lives. I recounted some of my adventures and misadventures. She shared her joy in being the mother to two wonderful girls. But she also expressed sadness in having missed out on a college education and the opportunity to explore her dreams.

When you have been close to someone and then are separated for a long time, sometimes the ability to communicate with one another goes away. Other times, it doesn't diminish at all. That was the case that day. Laura understood my feelings as well as anyone I had seen in years. And I think I understood her joy—and her sadness.

After our walk, saying goodbye was difficult. Years had passed since we had seen one another. We didn't know when or if we would see one another again. I drove away with a heavy heart.

I have not seen Laura since that day. But about five years after the visit, I had a phone conversation with Laura. She had taken her life back. She was in graduate school in women's studies.

Way to go Laura!

*****

Back on the road, my car was running perfectly. I was enjoying the quiet solitude of driving through the prairie country of southern Minnesota. I wondered what adventure would come next. Would I find roots and settle down in the next place I chose to live?

I thought about the advice given to me by my friend Raka while I was in college. Would I find that elusive *it* that he had referred to? Or would that magical objective elude me? And Raka had said I would recognize it when I found it. Would I?

I thought about that for a while; then sighed—and continued down the highway.

*****

I decided to drive straight through to Denver. By the time I got into Iowa and turned west onto Interstate 80, the trip had settled into a good rhythm. I picked up a couple of hitchhikers in western Iowa. They were also on their way to Denver and were thrilled to get a ride to their destination. I was pleased to have their company, especially since having someone to speak with would help me make sure I stayed wide-awake.

As the sun set in Nebraska, a radio station started playing a program of uninterrupted Beatles' hits. As I drove across the plains, the sky was full of stars, the Beatles classics came one right after another and my car ran perfectly. I was at peace.

*****

My Dodge Dart was getting over twenty-two miles per gallon. In 1974, that was outstanding. After I left the hitchhikers in a suburb east of Denver, I filled up my gas tank. I learned I had a problem. When I calculated mileage for that last tank, I found I was getting only fifteen miles per gallon. My peace of mind was quickly dissolved.

Two hours later, I pulled in front of my mom's home. I was tired, but glad to have safely completed the drive. After a warm welcome from my mom and brother, I took a long nap. When I got up from the nap, I unloaded the Dart. That was when I saw gasoline dripping from my gas tank.

I drove to a nearby auto repair shop. It didn't take the mechanic long to diagnose my problem. The bottom of my car, including the gas tank, had been driven for years over the salt used to melt ice on Minnesota highways. The gas tank was corroded. It needed to be repaired or replaced.

It hit me. I could not afford to continue owning a car. I had no flow of income. Carrying it a step beyond that, I just couldn't afford to keep that particular car. The Dodge Dart had become a deep sinkhole. That gas tank repair would be my final investment in the car. After I paid for its repair, I sold the Dart for seven hundred dollars.

The original purchase price plus all repairs totaled to more than two thousand four hundred dollars. My financial loss was a bummer. But, handing the keys over to its new owner brought immediate relief. And, as I referenced earlier, owning a Chrysler product had become an education in economics.

*****

When my mother and brother Johnny moved to San Francisco from Moorhead in 1967, my sister and I traveled cross country with them. We lived with them—for a while— in the apartment my mom rented on Nob Hill. However, during most of the seven years since, it had been my mother and brother by themselves. My mom had shown great courage in making a life for herself and Johnny. She established a career, bought a house and created many connections and routines that made life meaningful.

The visit to Denver was important. My grandparents, aunt and uncle, father, sister, brother-in-law, nephew and a slew of other relatives were coming to honor my brother. Johnny had turned into an incredibly bright and sweet young man. The week of his bar mitzvah was a festive time during which we all focused on Johnny. We were all so proud to celebrate his bar mitzvah, to let him know how much we cared.

However, the bar mitzvah came and went and family members departed to their various regions of the country. I had been the first visitor to arrive and was the last to leave. My mother tried to convince me to stay in Denver. But I knew I had not found what I was looking for. I needed to move on.

I wasn't sure what I should do or where I should go. I had been considering options ever since I decided to leave the Twin Cities. Taking a trip to Latin America seemed like an exciting adventure. I could visit my friends Madeleine and Matheus in Brasilia as well as my friend Fabio in Columbia. Taking that trip, I reasoned, certainly would not be running away from my life or its unresolved challenges. Or, if it would be, I repressed it.

*****

Before I headed to Latin America, I decided to visit Russ in Michigan. Sometimes it's important to have an opportunity to say your thoughts out loud. Visiting Russ would give me that sort of opportunity. And I was confident that Russ would give me honest feedback.

Russ was enrolled at the University of Michigan School of Medicine. He was spending the summer as an intern in Manistee, a small town in Western Michigan. Since I had no car to drive and did not have the emotional energy to take on a hitchhiking trip, I traveled by bus.

My visit in Manistee lasted only a few days. During that time, I got a chance to tell Russ what was happening in my life and hear what was happening in his. Russ' life was coming together. He was feeling good about his progress in medical school and happy to have a relationship with Rebecca, the woman who would become his life partner.

I tried to explain to Russ my plan for travel in Latin America. But as I listened to myself, I realized the trip just didn't make sense. Going abroad again was not a good next step. It wasn't a plan. It was the lack of a plan.

Russ, who knew me well, agreed.

So, if I was going to make another effort to establish myself in the United States, where should I go? I considered the cities in which I'd already lived. I decided I didn't want to go backwards. Returning to any of those of those places seemed like it would be just that.

My sister Diane had once told me that people on the east coast of the United States were more interesting. But people on the west coast had their act together. When I was ready to settle down, she suggested I go to the west coast. As Russ and I talked about my options, I recalled Diane's advice.

The first city I had considered moving to after graduating from college had been Seattle. I had been there and liked it. The was on the water; in a beautiful location; with mountains to its east and west. I had good memories of buying food at the Pike Street market and purchasing camping equipment at Recreational Equipment Incorporated. Russ suggested an alternative—Portland Oregon. Portland had developed a reputation as a hip city and was also in a beautiful location. Becky had almost convinced me to move there when we left Greensboro. Maybe she was there?

I decided I needed more information. Russ and I went to a local bookstore to see if there was a book with information about those two cities. The only book that described them both was a *Shell Guide* and the information in it was useless.

I am not sure what the deciding factor was, but I told Russ, "I'm going to Seattle."

*****

A day later, Russ borrowed a pickup truck and gave me a ride to a ferry boat terminal in Muskegon Michigan, a small city on the shores of Lake Michigan. I purchased a ferry boat ticket there to Milwaukee. Once I arrived in Milwaukee, I could catch Amtrak's Empire Builder to Seattle and start my new life.

My new life? I guess you've heard that from me before.

*****

The ferry boat was actually a large ship. Shortly after it headed into that great lake, I figured out why the boat was so large. Lake Michigan is enormous—it was like an ocean. For more than two hours during the crossing, I couldn't see land in any direction. Four hours after leaving Muskegon, the boat arrived in Milwaukee. The train station was a short bus ride from the ferry terminal.

A few hours later, I was on the Empire Builder traveling across Wisconsin. The train's route took me through Minneapolis, St. Paul, Fargo and Moorhead; then across North Dakota, Montana, Idaho and into Washington State.

I had no concerns about finding a place to live or a low-wage job. Experience had taught me those essentials would work out. So, I just sat back and enjoyed the train trip. I've always liked riding on trains. But this trip turned out to be the most pleasant rail trip of my life. I gazed out the window at a vast assortment of landscapes; read a compilation of science fiction short stories; chatted with people I met on the train; and ate in the elegance of the Empire Builder dining car, appreciating its wonderful food and reasonable prices. In fact, I had my first bowl of cream of broccoli soup on that trip. I loved it.

The highlight of the trip was a middle of the night ride in the scenic cruiser car. As the Empire Builder traversed the mountains and forests of Glacier National Park—I saw a large moose—in the moonlight—standing at the side of the train track—watching our train pass into the night.

I knew several people in Seattle.

One acquaintance from college, Tom, lived in Seattle's University District. I had written Tom informing him I would be coming to town; letting him know I hoped to spend a few days at his house while looking for an apartment.

After disembarking from the train in Seattle, I called Tom. I was welcomed. Yes—I could stay at his home until I found a place of my own. Three other Carleton graduates were renting rooms from him as they pursued post-graduate degrees at the University of Washington. One of those housemates was out of town. I had a room to myself for a few days.

Once I explored the city, I quickly decided to live on Seattle's Capitol Hill. Capitol Hill was the center of Seattle's counter culture, had excellent inexpensive restaurants, interesting shops, and residents of all colors and persuasions. It was walking distance from downtown Seattle and included Volunteer Park—forty acres of trees, fields, gardens, walking paths, museums, free rock concerts and an open-air theater. Capitol Hill also had modest priced apartments in buildings that reminded me of the classy 1920s vintage apartments of Detroit.

Tom and his housemates warned me that Capitol Hill was not a safe place to live. But after walking through it, I could see it was much safer than Detroit.

*****

I rented a furnished studio apartment for eighty-five dollars a month. In addition to being a short walking distance from Volunteer Park, I was two blocks away from the main bus line, a dozen blocks from downtown Seattle and just four blocks from the Capitol Hill Food Co-op.

I bought my standard set of used pots and pans at a Goodwill Store and started cooking vegetarian meals with foods purchased at the co-op. My favorite meal was pressure cooked brown rice and onions scooped on top of a sliced-up avocado. On top of that, I poured a small cup of homemade yogurt. I loved it. I think about that dish today and get hungry. (I had finally gotten down the principles of *Diet for a Small Planet*).

During the summer of 1974, my favorite television show was the Richard Nixon impeachment hearings. Since I didn't have a TV, I watched the spectacle at Snookie's Tavern, a pub two blocks from my apartment. I'd sit at the bar, order a schooner of beer (about fifty cents) and see Richard Nixon's presidency unravel. It was great entertainment. The main reason the Nixon impeachment has never become a miniseries is that the actual event was so entertaining. It would be difficult to beat.

I had saved enough money working at St. Paul's Children's Hospital to take a couple months off before looking for a job. During that summer of 1974, I enjoyed free theater, rock concerts and played pickup football games at

Volunteer Park. I also spent a lot of time walking around the city, getting to know it, coming to appreciate its charm.

*****

My cousin Jill—Harold and Joyce's middle child—moved to Seattle six months before I did. I hadn't seen Jill much since she was a little girl. But I got to know and enjoy her after arriving in Seattle. Seattle Community College (located on Capitol Hill) had one of the best American Sign Language training programs in the country. Jill had come to Seattle a year before because she had decided to become a translator for the deaf.

Having a relative nearby was a treat. Jill and I got together often, sharing memories of childhood. In late August of 1974, I got a really bad cold. Jill brought me a large batch of home-made avgolemono soup, a Greek soup made from egg, lemon juice and rice. Having somebody bring me a pot of soup when I was sick was a new luxury. I'll always treasure the memory of that avgolemono soup.

*****

A small house next to my apartment building was home for several older men who were poor and often didn't have enough to eat. One of them was named *Rainbow*. Rainbow was an African-American with a graying afro who dressed in old blue jeans and brightly colored dashikis. Whenever I saw Rainbow, he flashed a smile. I generally gave him a quarter or fifty cents.

It has always been interesting to me that people who have less money, as I did then, are often more generous in sharing what they have than those who have more money than they need.

*****

My hair was long—down to my shoulders. To brighten up my appearance, I often wore a head band. I turned my jeans into bellbottoms by opening the outside seam at the bottom of each leg. Then I sewed into each leg's open seam a section from a red cowboy bandana. My bellbottoms weren't as stylish as the Beatles' outfits in *The Yellow Submarine*. In fact, I probably looked a little like a clown. But I didn't know that and I felt cool.

*****

Seattle was culturally alive. OK. It wasn't Paris. But there were always cool things happening. I saw Henry Fonda at the Moore Theatre in a one-person play about the life of Clarence Darrow. I attended a George Harrison concert at the Seattle Center. Cinema was happening in Seattle. I joined the Seattle Film Society which showed old films in a church basement. I also went to films from the 1930s and 1940s at some of Seattle's small, old-time theaters that had been given new life by young hip owners.

*****

Moving from place to place over the prior few years had taken its toll. I woke up one night and couldn't figure out where I was living. I finally looked out my apartment window to see if there were any clues regarding my location. I saw a laundromat across the street and based upon the neon sign in its window, I concluded I was in an English-speaking country.

I enrolled in a free-university ballet course and relished it thoroughly even though I had no illusions about my dancing skills. I probably liked it primarily because I was the only guy in a class full of young attractive women.

But I never got a date from that venue.

*****

Through the free-university, I signed up for weekly visits to jail inmates at the State Prison in Monroe. Once a week, I rode to the penitentiary with three other class members. Visiting the prison was a fascinating opportunity to get to know extremely bright people who had messed up their lives.

Ranger, a twenty-year-old inmate, was serving time for bringing a gun—and using it—at a friend's court hearing. Ranger had definitely messed up his life. After fleeing the courthouse, he and his friend were pursued by police helicopters and squad cars in a chase that became a public spectacle when it was telecast live from a local television station's traffic helicopter.

Ranger played the guitar before being locked up. He didn't have a guitar in the prison. I decided he needed a guitar worse than I did. I gave him my guitar.

Ranger's father was in prison. So were his three brothers. One of his older brothers was also in the group of inmates we visited. That brother's crime was also unique. He had been drunk and in need of cash. He went into a restaurant to steal some money. Ranger's brother grabbed a handful of cash from an open cash register and ran out through what he thought was the back door. Unfortunately, the door led into the restaurant's pantry. Restaurant staff held the pantry door shut until the police arrived.

Listening to Ranger's brother describe his crime and punishment was entertaining. But his story spoke clearly of the difference between these brothers' lives and mine.

*****

It was the end of September and I had been in Seattle for two months. It was time to find work. The biggest department store in Seattle was The Bon Marche'. Its downtown store was the cornerstone of the downtown retail corridor. I went into the Bon's personnel office to ask if they had any openings. An hour and a half later, I exited as the downtown store's newest janitor. A couple of evenings later, I started work. Each night, I vacuumed, cleaned and waxed the second-floor women's wear department.

Janitors at the Bon only saw one another when we clocked in at the beginning of a shift, during our meal and coffee breaks and when we clocked out to go home. The janitorial supervisor treated all employees with the same level of respect—none. He made it clear he didn't trust any of us. After two weeks working as a janitor at the Bon, two things were evident. The first was why the Bon Marche' always had janitorial openings. The second was that I needed to find a different job.

*****

My apartment was four blocks from Recreational Equipment Incorporated—known to most customers as REI. REI had been formed in 1938 as a member owned Seattle cooperative. It sold quality hiking, climbing and camping gear. In 1969, when Russ and I hitchhiked to Seattle on our way to the Olympic Peninsula, I joined REI. After that, I purchased all of my camping gear from them by mail.

When I first applied for work at REI, the receptionist told me the store might have some openings coming up. She encouraged me to check back with her as often as I wanted. So, I went to the store almost every other day to see if any positions had opened. Each time I inquired, she responded in a gracious manner that no openings had been posted, but encouraged me to keep trying.

REI sold a lot of downhill and cross-country skis and ski boots. Toward the end of October, there was an opening for a ski mechanic—that's a technician who attaches bindings to skis. The receptionist asked me if I had any relevant skills. I responded enthusiastically—I did and couldn't imagine a more ideal job.

A couple of days later, I was interviewed by Riley. Riley had been with REI for more than a decade. He was their expert on attaching bindings to skis. Riley looked as Irish as his name sounds and had a positive, almost jolly manner. He explained that he needed a temporary employee just through the ski season. Then he led me down an old wooden stairway to his workshop in the store's basement— located next to the outdoor equipment merchandise—a mélange of ski equipment, sleeping bags, and other hiking equipment.

Riley offered me the job which I enthusiastically accepted. He told me that his team had fun, did its job well and was productive—in that order. He added that doing our job well was more important than the speed with which we completed it. His favorite phrase—which he repeated often—was *The hurrieder I go, the behinder I get.*

*****

On my first day at REI, Riley patiently showed me the tools I would use and demonstrated the care necessary when attaching bindings to skis.

Customers bought their skis, boots and bindings as a matched set. The bindings needed to be secured to the skis in exactly the right position to precisely fit the boot and support the height and weight of the skier. Ski mechanics drilled holes deep enough for the screws to secure the binding, but never so deep as to damage a ski's integrity or,

God forbid, to pierce through the bottom of the ski. Quality was a priority.

Riley preached, "Measure twice and cut once. If you do that," he would say, "your work will move forward more quickly and you will waste fewer materials." Since leaving REI, I have found many opportunities to apply and benefit from Riley's principles of quality. It is worth noting that they were not exactly the same as Chrysler's.

As we worked on pair after pair of skis and bindings, we listened to the sound of rock and roll on the radio and to stories from team members about outdoor adventures. The stories were often funny. Sometimes they turned into exciting and heroic wilderness adventures.

*****

Riley's crewmembers were mountain climbers, skiers, hikers and bicyclists. In fact, all REI employees excelled in at least one area of outdoor adventure and were able to give enthusiastic expert advice to store customers. I had never worked with such an engaging group. In addition to loving the outdoors, they were enthusiastic about life; enjoyed laughing; and regularly celebrated their camaraderie. I cannot remember an ill-tempered REI employee.

One of my most engaging co-workers was a sales clerk named Rod who sold hiking boots and sleeping bags. Rod had a sharp sense of humor—sometimes perhaps a little too sharp.

One day he came into our shop to share a funny, if perhaps disrespectful, interchange with a customer. Rod had been helping a woman who wanted to buy a sleeping bag. Being an intelligent, confident and thorough person, the woman kept asking more and more questions. (You know the type. They sat in the front of you in your high school history class and asked the teacher dumb questions in order to get brownie points). After a series of less than profound questions, the woman asked, "Can you tell me what the difference is between duck down and goose down?"

Rod paused—considered his options—then responded, "The biggest difference between the two is that ducks can run faster than geese".

The woman thought about his response and went ahead and purchased a goose down sleeping bag.

*****

My college acquaintance Tom, whose house had been my first base in Seattle, invited me to join him at a pot-luck Thanksgiving dinner hosted by a group of hip young people. Tom was not a close friend. While at times he had been cordial, he often was as self-centered and arrogant as anyone I'd ever known. In this instance, however, he appeared to be showing a gracious side. Since I had been dreading spending Thanksgiving by myself, I was quite pleased to accept his invitation.

My contribution to the Thanksgiving feast would be a very healthy, home-made pumpkin pie. Instead of using commercially canned pumpkin, I bought a small pumpkin at the co-op, baked it and then, before adding eggs, canned milk, spices and honey, I slowly mashed the pumpkin with a fork creating a thick and somewhat stringy puree. The crust was made with stone-ground whole-wheat flour and butter. When it came out of the oven, the pie, looked a little crude. But I knew it would be healthy.

Before picking me up at two o' clock, Tom had said he would be working in his university laboratory.

At two, I was standing in front of my apartment building, holding my pumpkin pie and waiting for Tom. He was late. But I was patient. By three, I had become a little less patient. I went up to my apartment to wait for him to buzz me. At four, I was angry—and hungry. I ate my pumpkin pie. (It was probably healthy, but did not taste very good).

At a little after five, Tom showed up. He had a big smile on his face. The work at his biochemistry lab had gone very well. He was so pleased with how much work he had completed that it hadn't occurred to him that picking me up three hours late might, in any way, be an issue. Egotism is such an incredibly pure and insulating characteristic!

I swallowed my pride and went with him to the potluck dinner. It was good I'd eaten my pie because all of the other pot luck food had been eaten.

That was my all-time most unpleasant Thanksgiving.

*****

Many things were special about working at REI. An old REI Christmas tradition was for staff on Christmas Eve Day to bring a bottle of hard liquor to work. In the afternoon, employees would walk around the store, from department to department, and have their glass filled, courtesy of the department they were visiting. I understand how problematic that was from a risk management perspective, but that being said, it was joyful. I have fond memories of that afternoon.

A memo was sent out by management a couple of days later informing all REI employees that the long-time tradition of departments hosting employees with hard liquor would not be allowed again.

Progress has its price.

*****

I had never gone downhill skiing. My co-workers encouraged me to try. I agreed to go. So, one evening after work, I rode with my co-workers to a ski resort at a mountain pass about forty miles east of Seattle. REI lent skis and boots to employees at no cost. So, my only expenditure for the evening was a lift ticket.

My co-workers gave me some skiing pointers—you know—how to turn and how to stop. I began my skiing adventure on a short gentle run. On those shallow slopes, skiing seemed pretty easy. After a while, I tried the medium slopes. They went pretty well too. My confidence and skills were growing. This wasn't that hard. I reveled in the beauty and camaraderie of the ski slopes.

Being a fairly athletic person who enjoys physical challenges, I decided to go ahead and try the steep slope. As I rode the chairlift to the top of the run, I watched skiers below me expertly craft their way down the slope. I was totally enthused.

After getting off of the chairlift, I quickly learned that steep hills are different than more gradual slopes and that slaloming back-and-forth requires skill—something I had somehow neglected to develop. I also came to realize how fast one can move on skis when one heads straight down a slope—like a bat out of hell. By the time I got to the bottom of the hill, I was fortunate to be in one piece and not to have injured anyone else.

However, my lack of skill was not unique. It was evident that other skiers had no idea what they were doing. At one point as I skied down the hill, another dangerously out-of-control skier almost hit me. As I quickly adjusted my course to get out of the way of that human bullet, somebody yelled down from a chairlift, "Nice dodge!"

After that evening, I resolved that if I continued to ski, I would either end up seriously injuring myself or killing someone else. I have not gone downhill skiing since.

*****

John Nyren, a friend from college, had approached his post-Carleton life in a manner somewhat similar to me. We'd crossed paths a couple of times since graduation. But in 1974, I had no idea where John was living. In those days, the best way to locate someone who you'd lost touch with was by calling the phone company long distance information operator and getting lucky.

I knew John's parents had once lived in Silver Springs, Maryland. I called information there. The operator informed me there was no John Nyren nor any Nyrens listed in Silver Springs. But, the operator added, there was a listing for a Nyren in a nearby suburb. I took that phone number and hoped I would be lucky.

When I called the number, a young woman answered the phone. I asked her if John Nyren was there. She said, "John isn't living in Washington DC. John lives in Washington State!" (How dumb of me, really).

The woman was John's sister. She informed me that John was living in Bellingham—a hundred miles north of Seattle. He didn't have a phone, but she gave me his street address. I wrote to John and he responded quickly, welcoming a visit from me. The following weekend, I went to Bellingham. During the next few months, John and I got together several times. It was nice to see an old friend and John knew a variety of coeds at a university in Bellingham.

We visited them in their dorm rooms and shared a pot of tea or bowl of popcorn.

*****

I met a young man named Gordon Allen. I remember his name well because he was named after two ancestors, both Confederate commanding officers in the Civil War: General John B. Gordon and Major William Allen.

Gordon lived in a classic old Victorian house on Capitol Hill. Its 87-year-old owner had seven other renters, all women in their sixties. The house had elegant staircases with polished dark cherry banisters, oak hardwood floors, thick oriental carpets and several stained-glass windows. Its living room, a common area for house residents, was elegantly furnished with early twentieth century furniture that Mr. Mallory, the house's owner and his wife had probably purchased when the house, the furniture and their marriage were all new.

Gordon's rent for his room was fifty dollars a month. That was quite a bit less than I was spending. I asked him if there were any other rooms for rent in the house. He told me one small room was available. I spoke with Mr. Mallory and learned the room's rent was forty-five dollars a month. The room was on the second floor of the three-story home and shared a bathroom with several other people. It was furnished with a twin bed, a chest of drawers, a hotplate and a small closet. The room had once been the large closet for the home's master bedroom. While the room may have been small, it was pleasant and had every feature I needed.

In a matter of days, I moved from my apartment into Mr. Mallory's home.

*****

1975 arrived. My life was in pretty good order. I was working at a job with people I liked. I had an inexpensive room in a beautiful neighborhood and a few friends. I began to feel like I was establishing those roots I sought.

However, by the end of January, the number of skis sold by REI declined and, along with that, so did my workload. Reality struck—my position was temporary. In early February, Riley informed me I was being laid off. He told me that when the bicycle season got going, he might be able to hire me again as a seasonal bicycle mechanic. That seemed like an attractive option. But it would be at least a month before that temporary position would be available.

I liked Seattle and did not want to move away. Instead, I decided to take a break. Greyhound Bus had a special fare called the *Discovery Pass*. It allowed unlimited Greyhound Bus travel throughout the United States for a one-month period. A ticket cost only one hundred and fifty dollars.

After being laid off, the first thing I did was apply for unemployment compensation. The second was to purchase a Greyhound Discovery Pass. I would travel around the country to visit family members and friends.

The trip was satisfying. I enjoyed visiting my grandparents in Minneapolis. It was good to see Karen in Chicago. She had a boyfriend and was enrolled in graduate school. I visited Russ in Ann Arbor. Russ was continuing to progress in medical school. I saw my father in New York. As always, he graciously welcomed me. Then I visited my sister in Chapel Hill. After that, I took the long cross-country ride to Denver where I was able to catch up with my mom and brother. Each friend and family member treated me well. But I was eager to return to Seattle.

*****

It was the beginning of March 1975. I had scratched my travel itch. I was back in my room in Mr. Mallory's house totally committed to building a life in Seattle—and full of hope for the future.

16—Finding It

The day after I returned, I trooped over to REI, hopeful that I'd be hired as a bicycle mechanic on Riley's crew. With some luck, I might even be able to move into a regular ongoing job at the co-op.

However, REI hadn't yet opened any summer jobs. So, I had to be patient.

I hadn't received any unemployment compensation. Children's Hospital in St. Paul told the Washington State Department of Employment Security that I had been a Children's Hospital employee for less than three months. If that had been true, I would not have qualified for unemployment compensation. I figured the confusion would be resolved quickly since I had worked at Children's for almost eight months. In the interim, I managed my expenses and savings carefully.

*****

I visited John in Bellingham. On an evening Greyhound trip back to Seattle, I sat next to a young woman who was also returning to Seattle from Bellingham. She told me she had spent all of her cash and hadn't eaten supper. When the bus pulled into the Mount Vernon depot, I gave her a dollar to call her roommate who would meet her when the bus arrived in Seattle. I told her to keep the change and buy an ice cream sandwich. She thanked me and took my phone number.

A few days later, I received a phone call from her. She and her roommate were going to have a party to celebrate both her roommate's birthday and the vernal equinox—the first day of spring. I gladly accepted her invitation.

*****

As I rode a city bus to the party, I decided I just wanted to have fun. For once, I wasn't going to worry about finding the love of my life—I would just enjoy the evening.

As I walked from the bus, I heard a stereo blaring rock and roll music when I was still a half block away from the party. As I climbed the steep steps to the Victorian duplex's front door, I saw a bunch of hip young people through a living room window. This was going to be a great party!

Upon entering the house, the woman who had invited me introduced me to her roommate, Carol. Carol welcomed me and told me drinks were in the kitchen. As I entered the kitchen, somebody passed me a joint and I took a couple of drags, then poured a glass of white wine and went into the living room. The music was blaring and people were dancing. I asked somebody to dance and danced with her until she said she wanted to get a drink. Then, I asked somebody else to dance. I was high, enjoying the music and having fun dancing. It was a good party.

I asked a tall, very stylish woman if she wanted to dance. She told me she really didn't like dancing but would enjoy talking with me. Since I was having fun dancing, I told her, "No thanks." She went into the kitchen and I asked another young woman to dance.

This woman was medium height, had long blonde hair and large tan plastic hoop earrings. Her eyes were made up with sky-blue eye shadow in an intense Cleopatra style. The woman was wearing blue jeans and a white peasant-style cotton blouse. She liked dancing as much as I did. We danced for half an hour. The living room was getting warm. We each took a glass of wine out onto a large second-floor balcony to get some fresh air. As we approached the balcony, people shared joints with us.

The woman's name was Marsha. Marsha started telling me why men were such a pain in the ass. I can't remember her specific complaints because I was pretty stoned. But I listened patiently. After about ten minutes, she seemed to be finished with her complaints about men being creeps. So, I asked, "Would you like to dance some more?"

She was game. She had gotten the things that bothered her about men off of her chest. We went back to living room and continued to dance and enjoy the music.

I can't remember why or how, but we started speaking French to one another. Throughout the evening, we spoke French, danced and listened to the music. Marsha asked me how old I was. I told her that I was twenty-five. She responded that I was so young. She was an older woman. She was twenty-eight!

*****

As the party began to die down, Marsha asked me if I needed a ride home. I said yes, I did. She told me she needed to give her friend Eia a ride home first. Eia turned out to be the tall stylish woman who wanted to talk rather than dance. As Marsha drove Eia to her home, Eia said to me, "I'm sorry. I can't remember your name."

I told her my name and went on to explain how easy it is to forget a person's name.

Before we pulled out of Eia's driveway, Marsha turned to me and said, "What's my name?"

After a pregnant pause, I took a shot. "Carol?"

Marsha replied, "No. My name is Heidi."

*****

Marsha drove me back to my house; came up to my room; and ended up spending the night. She had to get up early the next morning because she needed to pick up her son who had spent the night with a friend. I made sure I got Marsha's phone number and gave her the Mallory house phone number.

I had gone to a party with the intent of just enjoying myself and ended up meeting someone I really liked.

*****

A few days later, I called Marsha and asked her if she and her son wanted to have dinner with me. She accepted. But her son, Sean, couldn't come. He was visiting his dad in Eugene Oregon. A couple of days later, Marsha came over to my room. I fixed my rice, onion, avocado and yogurt dish and we drank a good bottle of Chardonnay.

One of my favorite films, *Amarcord* by Federico Fellini, was playing at a local Capitol Hill theater. *Amarcord* is Fellini's recollections of his childhood, growing up in fascist Italy. The film is an unusual mix of beauty and violence. Its visually stunning images are presented with dreamlike music. Marsha loved it. She told me it reminded her of her favorite Fellini film, *Juliet of the Spirits*. After watching *Amarcord*, we walked down Broadway and had a dessert of dark chocolate mousse at an elegant restaurant.

It was a lovely weekend.

*****

Marsha was an only kid raised in Riverside, California. Her father had spent all of World War II on the front lines in Africa and Europe. The war took it out of him. Once he returned to the States, he worked in a variety of blue-collar jobs, but never earned a lot. Marsha's parents were mildly, but happily dysfunctional. The small family lived with Marsha's grandfather in her grandfather's tiny home.

After two years of junior college in Riverside, Marsha went to the University of California at Long Beach for her junior year of college. She met Ray there. Ray was an artist who believed in himself above everything else. When Ray proposed to Marsha, it was her ticket away from home. She didn't hesitate to accept.

Within a year, they had a child and had moved to Eugene so Ray could pursue his passion for creating sculpture. Marsha was an artist as well. But it was clear to Ray that he was the great artist. Within a couple of years, Ray moved out of their cottage into an art studio so that he could pursue his art unfettered by others. Greatness has its sacrifices—generally of others.

Soon afterwards, Marsha and Ray separated and she moved to Seattle.

*****

Marsha was employed as an advertising agency art director. She owned a car and had a child. I had never gone out with anyone so traditionally grounded. But Marsha enjoyed life and cared deeply about many of the things that were important to me.

When Marsha moved to Seattle, she was involved with a designer who fancied himself the second coming of Frank Lloyd Wright. Probably the primary quality this guy had in common with Frank Lloyd Wright was arrogance. His loss was my gain. Marsha was extremely honest, straightforward and didn't play games.

I'd never met anyone as honest as she. A lot of times when people try to be honest, they also end up being unkind.

That could not be said about her. She treated others with kindness and respect—hoping they would return the favor.

Marsha and Sean lived in a five hundred square-foot house in the center of Seattle's Rainier Valley, the tough inner city of Seattle. She lived there because she could afford it. She didn't drive her car a lot because its tires were bald.

Marsha liked to sing acapella. I enjoyed listening. We would sit on the front steps of her rented house with a glass of wine on a warm evening. She would close her eyes and sing sad ballads with passion. She appreciated the richness in life; loved color and design; and enjoyed diverse styles in visual and music arts. I remember her telling me that even before she learned to read, she could find the Egyptian section in her parents' encyclopedia.

*****

A week after I took Marsha to see *Amarcord*, Sean was back from his dad's. Marsha invited me to supper. I met her near her office in Pioneer Square. We rode the bus, getting off about five blocks from her house. We needed to pick up Sean at the babysitters.

It was the first time I had met Sean. Marsha told me later that Sean reacted differently to me then he had to her other men friends. Generally, he was excited to turn a guy into a new playmate. When I first met Sean, he was a little distant. Marsha figured that perhaps he felt a little threatened. After we got home, Sean loosened up. Dinner was chicken enchiladas. Growing up in Southern California, Marsha had learned to cook many wonderful Mexican dishes. It was a fun and tasty meal.

*****

As we saw more of one another, Marsha made clear her feeling of vulnerability. She had been consistently put down and ignored by her husband and had regularly heard from her last boyfriend about the wonderful qualities of his previous girlfriend. She worried about how much I liked her—whether I would leave her for somebody else. I told her more than once, "Don't worry about me being dishonest or leaving you for someone else. If you want to worry, worry about me moving on to the next city."

My leaving Seattle was a realistic possibility. If she needed to fret about something, it would be less painful to worry about me being a flake than a guy who left her for another woman.

*****

Pioneer Square was the oldest district in Seattle. With redevelopment, it had become Seattle's hip area. Marsha's advertising agency, The Creative Department, was one of the first companies to move into the renovated area. Her colleagues were fairly hip and deeply proud of it.

Before going up to Marsha's office, I sometimes would pick up a bouquet of flowers at the flower shop on the ground floor of her building. She told me afterwards that her co-workers were impressed with the flowers I brought but were taken aback by my long hair and un-businesslike demeanor. While the office prided itself in being hip, I made them feel uncomfortable.

*****

A few weeks after we got together, Marsha, Sean and I drove up to Bellingham to visit John. It was a fun stay. I enjoyed introducing John to Marsha and Sean.

We had an important conversation as we drove back. It was one of those talks that led to my saying, "You don't need to worry about me sneaking around and getting involved with another woman. If you want to worry about something, worry about me moving to another city."

I guess I had used that line once too often. Marsha broke down crying and said, with a great deal of passion, "But I want to have a long-term relationship."

How does one respond to that?

*****

I continued to check in at REI about job vacancies. I finally realized they were not going to hire me. And, letters from the State Office of Unemployment Compensation informed me that Children's Hospital in Seattle was continuing to insist I'd worked for them for less than three months.

So, I spent my money carefully and continued to enjoy life. I often went to the Seattle library and checked out materials on things that I just found interesting. I checked out books on history, science and nature.

I had seen a lot of butterflies around Seattle, but didn't know too much about them. Butterflies seemed like creatures that were beautiful and did no harm. I needed to know more. So, I checked out a book on butterflies. It was fascinating.

I checked out books on gardening. I had never gardened—but I was interested in it. I asked Marsha if I could start a garden in her backyard. She said "Sure". I purchased ten yards of rich soil (making sure it had all of the minerals and nutrients that I had read about) and had it delivered to her backyard. We planted a vegetable garden.

*****

Before I graduated from college, I'd gone hiking and camping with Russ along the Lake Ozette trail near the coastline of the Olympic Peninsula. I told John about the beautiful walk through the rainforest and along the untamed shoreline. He was enthusiastic about making the trip.

It seemed like a good time for a break. I didn't know how to proceed in my relationship with Marsha. I was afraid—not sure if I should be making a commitment. I didn't want to hurt Marsha. But I didn't want to hurt myself either.

The hiking trip would give me an opportunity to figure out what I should do next.

*****

John and I caught the State Ferry out of downtown Seattle to Bainbridge Island. We hitchhiked on a two-lane highway across Bainbridge, over the Hood Canal Bridge, and then through the rich forested lands of the Olympic Peninsula. We arrived at the Lake Ozette and Olympic Coast trailhead in the late afternoon. We immediately began the three-mile hike to the coast. The trail passes a stunning wilderness lake, goes along and then crosses a small river on a hanging wooden bridge. The trail continues through an old growth forest, past marshlands, into the rain forest and finally onto the coastline—the last wild seashore in this country.

I was carrying a backpack, food for several meals, a small stove, cooking equipment, my sleeping bag and a tent. John had a sleeping bag and a bag of nuts. He told me he didn't need to carry more supplies because he was happy sleeping under the stars and the bag of nuts was all the food he needed. He would be willing to share my tent, but it wasn't necessary. He also was agreeable to sharing my food. But he would be happy with just his nuts. I was carrying thirty pounds of camping equipment and food. John was carrying five.

We got to the coast just before sunset and found a nice campsite. I set up my tent, cooked dinner and we turned in. The next morning, we got up early. I fixed oatmeal and coffee. Then we set off on our way down the coast. It was picturesque. On our right, strewn across the rocky seashore, were mountains of logs from flotillas that had broken loose during huge Pacific storms. On our left was a magnificent old-growth rain forest. The only sounds we heard were those of the wind blowing through the trees and the waves crashing down on the beach.

Since John was carrying a lot less than me, he moved faster. Before long, John was out of sight. By noon, I had no idea of how far ahead he was. But I was ready to have lunch—and angry at his self-centered attitude. I found a campsite where I not only fixed my lunch, I put up my tent.

I was fuming.

Over the next hour or so, as I ate my lunch and drank a cup of tea, hikers coming north would ask me, "Are you Roger?" When I told them I was, they said, "John is waiting for you about a mile ahead. He asked us to let you know."

I figured that was John's problem, not mine. I responded, "Okay. Thanks."

Finally, reason got the better me. I packed up my tent, loaded my backpack and started walking south—at my own pace—to meet John. I found him sitting by the trail. He'd already eaten a bunch of nuts for lunch. We continued our hike down the trail for another couple of hours and then set up the tent for the night.

The following morning, we had coffee and oatmeal, then started out on the trail. I remember noting that it was

June 21st, the summer solstice. I explained to John that because I was carrying more camping gear, I couldn't keep up with him. He agreed to move more slowly. We found a compromise pace. But John continued to lead as we moved along the trail.

*****

The trail narrowed into a path that straddled the crest of a hillside of rocks, cascading all the way down to the ocean shore. I was moving as fast as I could. Suddenly, it felt like two invisible hands had taken the top of my backpack and wrenched it to the right, throwing me down, off the path, onto the rocks. As I flew through the air and before I landed on the rocks, I heard a voice in my mind say, "You only live once. If something comes along, and you pass it up, you might not get that opportunity again."

John had seen me fall from the path and was concerned. He rushed back asking me if I was okay. As I stood up, I said. "Yes. I'm okay. But John, we're going back to Seattle. I'm moving in with Marsha".

*****

We got back on the trail and hiked another mile south. There, we found another trail that led us to the highway. A couple of hours later, we were on Highway 101, hitchhiking back to Seattle.

It was a beautiful northwest day—a soft light rain was mixed with occasional brilliant sunlight. As we got closer to Bainbridge Island, I started seeing rainbows— many of them.

I've always felt that rainbows are an important sign. As we hitchhiked, we didn't talk a lot. I was focused on getting back to Seattle and moving forward with my life.

John was aware of my serious state of mind and was respectful of it.

We got to the Bainbridge Island ferry terminal at around 6:30 in the evening. I tried to call Marsha from the pay phone at the Bainbridge Island ferry terminal. Her line was busy. I kept trying until it was time for the ferry to depart. Each time her line was busy.

We boarded the ferry. Ordinarily I would sit inside the ferry boat's main cabin with most of the other passengers. But that evening, I stood out on the deck at the front of the boat with my eyes on the Seattle skyline.

The ferry moved out of Bainbridge Island's Eagle Harbor, into Puget Sound and approached the City of Seattle. As we crossed Puget Sound, I saw rainbows on both sides of our ferry boat. I had never seen so many rainbows at once. Suddenly, I saw something that I had never seen before and have not seen since. The ferry, which was moving through a combination of sunlight and mist, passed through one end of a rainbow. I was surrounded by, and immersed in, the colors of the rainbow. Without intending to be metaphorical, I literally had reached the end of my rainbow.

The unusual beauty and symbolic power of that moment were not missed by John or me. This was a special day.

*****

John was a good friend. He was happy for me. When the ferry boat landed, I said goodbye to him. He headed for the Greyhound station to return to Bellingham. I went to a phone booth and called Marsha.

This time, Marsha answered the phone right away.

I asked, "Can you pick me up at the ferry terminal? We're back from our trip." I paused for a moment before adding, "And, I'm going to move in with you."

She told me she would be there in fifteen minutes.

Fifteen minutes was not too long to wait.

It had been a long journey.